THE AGE HERESY

For Sal,

You can be a Phoenix and rise from the ashes to re-generate yourself. We are all getting older, but with meta-positive thinking, we can realise our real potential. It is never too late to really LIVE life, and make the very most of it and ourselves!

I hope you enjoy this book – I think you will relate to a lot of the concepts contained therein.

Think Positive Thoughts! Always, Val xxx

THE AGE HERESY

You Can Achieve More – Not Less – As You Get Older

TONY BUZAN &
RAYMOND KEENE

Foreword by Jean Buzan

EBURY PRESS

First published in 1996

1 3 5 7 9 10 8 6 4 2

The authors and publisher are grateful to Ted Hughes for permission to reproduce the poem on pp.160–2.

Mind Maps™ is a registered trademark of the Buzan Organization.

First published in the United Kingdom in 1996 by
Ebury Press
an imprint of Random House
20 Vauxhall Bridge Road, London SW1V 2SA.

Random House Australia (Pty) Limited,
20 Alfred Street, Milsons Point, Sydney,
New South Wales 2061, Australia.

Random House New Zealand Limited,
18 Poland Road, Glenfield,
Auckland 10, New Zealand.

Random House South Africa (Pty) Limited,
PO Box 337, Bergvlei, South Africa.

Random House UK Limited Reg. No. 954009

ISBN 0 0918 5150 5

Managing editor: Mandy Greenfield
Designer: Nigel Partridge
Jacket design: Senate
Graphs: Anthony Duke
Printed and bound in Great Britain by BPC

CONTENTS

DEDICATION

THE AUTHORS DEDICATE THIS BOOK TO JEAN BUZAN, IN
HONOUR OF HER INTELLIGENCE, WISDOM, OUTSTANDING
PERSONAL EXAMPLE AND ONGOING CONTRIBUTION TO THE
FIELD OF GERONTOLOGICAL STUDIES.

ACKNOWLEDGEMENTS

The authors would like to thank the following individuals who have contributed to this volume, materially, with their ideas, assistance or expertise: Radiant-Thinking Instructor Bridget Phillips; International Chess Master Byron Jacobs and World Chess Federation Master Andrew Kinsman of *Use Your Head* magazine; Grand Master Mind Mapper Vanda North; Rikki Hunt; Professor Ben Zander; Jean Buzan; Professor Barry Buzan; John Naisbitt; World Memory Champion Dominic O'Brien; Sir Brian Tovey; Lady Mary Tovey; Dr Andrew Strigner; Professor Marvin Minsky of MIT; Dr Diana Woodruff; Professor Nathan Divinsky of the University of British Columbia; Jean Sewell; Julian Shuckburgh and Margaret Little; Louise Betwin and the staff of Prontaprint, Lavender Hill, London; Lesley Bias and Sandy Zambaux; David Cleaves and Tom Benning; Anna Sanderson, Nicky Thompson and Mandy Greenfield; Mike and Nusa Gelb, author and artist respectively. And special acknowledgement to Lady Mary for her Mind Maps.

And extra special thanks to 'Brain' Clivaz, General Manager of top London restaurant and Mecca of the Mind, Simpson's-in-the-Strand, for inviting the authors to hold their symposium, 'The Methuselah Mandate', in front of a VIP audience at his establishment in April 1995.

TONY BUZAN
RAYMOND KEENE

> ## BRAIN FLASH
>
> ### DESIGN YOUR OWN AGEING PROCESS
> *'Ageing is not identical with fate; individuals play a major role in designing their own process of ageing.'*

FOREWORD
by Jean Buzan, MA (born 1916)

———

'You're not getting older, you're getting better!'

Prevailing Delusions

Many of us still believe the widespread delusions about our mental capacity declining as we age. Do you still think that your brain cells die off daily throughout your life? That your brain power diminishes as you age, until finally, if you live long enough, you decline into 'senility'?

I did for many years, and if you do, then join a club of billions.

It isn't that the 'experts' deliberately misled us – they really believed what they were saying. The story goes that, at a post-mortem years ago, two young doctors remarked that, in general, older people's brains weighed a little less than those of younger people. 'That accounts for their failing mental capacities,' remarked one. From this reasonable, but unscientific, deduction, the assumption became an accepted 'fact'.

The story may be apocryphal, but the theory that we lose millions of brain cells on a continuing basis has been widely accepted for years. And, to too great an extent, it still is.

Change Your Life

The recently discovered truth is far more palatable, and knowing it can change a person's whole life.

First, our minds/intellect/intelligence do not consist of a limited number of brain 'cells', which die daily and cannot be renewed. The abilities of that incredible 3½-lb (1.6-kg) computer in your head are produced by the number of interconnections made between those cells. And that number, dear brain owner, is infinite in its growth potential!

So, you ask, what about the reduction in weight at post-mortems? I would propose that this is due merely to the overall reduction in body fluid as one ages physically. I would also propose that it is not inevitable. After all, how many of us really drink eight glasses of water daily, as we are exhorted to do?

There was another, more serious reason why this delusion was so widely accepted. When IQ testing first began, psychologists carried out studies comparing older and younger groups, and 'proved' that the latter were far more intelligent. QED: mental functioning declines with age.

These studies were known as cross-sectional and were carried out in a very simple fashion – in fact too simple! Two groups, one of older people and one of younger, were each given a time-limited IQ test. Since the younger groups consistently performed better than the older groups, the conclusion was that a person's intellectual capacity must, therefore, deteriorate with age.

CHANGE THE THINKING

Then some bright psychologist tried removing the time limit. The older people took a little longer, but gained appreciably improved results, quite comparable with those of the younger groups. The extra time needed was accounted for by two facts – the older people were unfamiliar with the type of tests used, which were commonplace to younger people; and the older peoples' brains contained more years of experience and therefore had more information to process when considering the questions.

YOU AGAINST YOURSELF

Eventually, psychologists devised the longitudinal type of test, whereby they tested a person annually for many years, comparing the results of the same people against themselves. And guess what? In many ways their results improved over the years.

Think what this exciting new information means. Providing that you believe in yourself, and continue to stimulate your brain, it really is true that 'You're not getting older, you're getting better!'

JEAN BUZAN

THE POWER OF FREE WILL

Professor David Suzuki is a geneticist at the University of Columbia. He has persuasively argued that although genes do play a fundamental role in determining human character, 'The really important genes are not the ones which tell us what to do, but the ones that give us the ability to change behaviour in response to our environment.'

In other words, there are genes that create what we recognize as free will. He claims that the whole evolution of higher mammals is the story of genes handing over control to the brain, so that people have become more and more capable of behaving independently of their genes.

The contradiction between free will and determinism is one that has run throughout philosophical debate from early times to our own, taking on different forms at different stages. The philosopher Spinoza, for example, in his work *Ethics,* articulated the argument that there is no such thing as free will and that circumstances are ruled by absolute logical necessity; everything that happens is a manifestation of God's nature, and it is logically impossible that events should be other than they are. Other philosophers were less happy with this rigidly deterministic framework, one that seems to place us in a clock-work universe, where 'God' releases the spring at the start of time and we all shuffle along predetermined paths, until that spring finally winds down.

A different aspect of this argument is the 'Nature v. Nurture' debate. Are we all little more than a distillation of the genetic material of our forebears, or are we capable of being moulded by the influences to which we are exposed in our own environment? Those of a deterministic inclination would probably argue that the most accurate indicator of human potential is the genetic hand dealt to them at conception, and that there is little that can be done to alter this. Clearly, and particularly in terms of physical development, this is going to be an important factor: if the parents are both below average height, their offspring is unlikely to become a basketball champion. In terms of mental development, however, the brain is capable of assimilating phenomenal amounts of information and, the more it is stimulated, the more it will have the potential to achieve at any age! In Chapter Four, for example, we introduce the exceptionally important TEFCAS model, with its emphasis on your ability to change and adjust.

In this book the authors explore the growing body of information that supports the theory that the brain thrives on stimulation. The more it gets, the more powerfully it evolves — at every stage of its development.

POTENTIAL LEONARDOS

Every human being is a potential Leonardo da Vinci!

Even the great Renaissance sculptor, Michelangelo, described his work as merely 'freeing the image that already existed inside the block of stone'. It is possible to view ongoing human development in the same terms.

If you use your brain as it should be used — and the authors map out an appropriate strategy in this book — the potential for developing your brain is limitless.

TONY BUZAN AND RAY KEENE

BRAIN FLASH

VITAL FACTORS IN AGEING GRACEFULLY

'History offers ample instances of brilliance in life's later years, from Michelangelo to Martha Graham.

The key factors include:

☆ **Staying socially involved.** Among those who decline, deterioration is most rapid in older people who withdraw from life.

☆ **Being mentally active.** Well-educated people who continue their intellectual interests tend to increase their verbal intelligence through old age.

☆ **Having a flexible personality.** A study found that people most able to tolerate ambiguity and enjoy new experiences in middle age maintained their mental alertness best through old age.

The new view is accompanied by data attacking the notion that the brain degenerates precipitously with ageing. The widespread belief that there is devastating cell loss in the elderly brain — and the related claim that each drink of liquor destroys a large number of brain cells — seems now to be unfounded. Marion Diamond, a neuroanatomist at the University of Berkeley, tried to track down the source of the belief and could find no definitive study proving it.'

SWIMMING RECORDS PROVE THAT AGE IS NO BARRIER TO SPEED

November 1995 statistics from the World Masters Swimming Division show that the men's record in the 50 metres Freestyle 35–39 years old section is 23.25 seconds; 55–59 years 27.05 seconds, and 80–84 years 34 seconds. The physical decline with age is amazingly small. Women's records are on average 5 seconds slower at all stages, but maintain a similarly small rate of decline.

INTRODUCTION

'No one under the age of 40 is permitted to read my book.'
Maimonides (AD 1135–1204) on his book *A Guide for the Perplexed*

'Everyone, from 8 to 118 and beyond, is positively encouraged to read our book.'
Tony Buzan, psychologist, and Ray Keene, Chess Grand Master, AD 1996

INTRODUCTION

The Age Heresy is aimed primarily at the generation now in their forties and fifties, the so-called baby-boomers, who form such a massive global presence in the world's developed nations. However, we are also addressing the over-fifties who still have serious ambitions to succeed. Of course, any book that gives advice on improving mental powers can be equally applicable to an 8-year-old or an 80-year-old, **or even a 118-year-old!** It is never too early, or too late, to start.

The core of the book is practical advice aimed directly at you, the reader, targeting your aspirations for the future, as well as your fears, and proposing solutions. You undoubtedly want to know what you can do to extend your physical and mental fitness beyond middle age, to resist the onslaught of younger generations and to reverse the negative stereotypes you standardly encounter, such as 'experience is no substitute for youthful energy and adaptability'. In short, you want to maximize your personal potential and **not be thrown on the scrapheap** simply because the years are gathering pace.

We illustrate our advice with shining examples of superlative achievements in great age — anecdotes of this nature spice and pepper the text to inspire you. Our book does three things:

1. It strikes a resounding note with the ageing population worldwide. It

addresses your issues with a clarion call that you cannot ignore and will instantly recognize as your own.

2. It offers a host of ideas for stimulating your brain, motivating you to stay fit and healthy. Remember: the more you stimulate yourself, the more you will be capable of achieving.

3. It reinforces the message with real-life precedents showing what can be achieved by those who start on the path to success later in life: for instance, by those who have only truly learnt how to learn, or how to think for themselves, well

> ### BRAIN FLASH
>
> #### THE COSTLY LAMENT OF BRITAIN'S DISCARDED 50-SOMETHINGS
>
> *'This year, many of my friends are reaching 50. One or two, riding high in affluence and achievement, are holding good parties. But their guests reveal a different story. For many more, the half-century is bringing an end to careers they thought would go on a lot longer and, they hoped, further. To their amazement, they are cast as the fat being shed in the latest corporate diet plan. Some are victims of multinationals' mass culls of middle-rank executives, when age is often the first parameter fed into the search programme. Professionals, sidelined from the fee-earning mainstream to make way for young bloods, find they are an embarrassment when 1980s' overheads have to be cut. A generation of nearly-men — and it is usually men — are falling off the corporate pyramid.'*

past the end of their formal school or college education. And we record the exploits of those who have made, or continue to make, their mark in great age. Such inspirational examples include the 100-year-old Australian grandmother who broke a swimming record, and the self-defence of the 80-year-old Greek dramatist Sophocles against his son's predatory law suit.

ORIGINS IN GENIUS

Time and again, during our decades-long research into the great minds of the past and present, we have been struck by the extraordinary force, vigour, ambition and sheer drive exhibited by people at an age when human beings are conventionally meant to slow down. Now, more than ever before in previous societies, there is a cult of youth and a tendency to throw 50- (or even 40-) somethings on the scrapheap to make way for the young.

Yet everything we learnt from the great minds we studied in depth contradicted this piece of conventional modern wisdom. We also noted, amazingly, that the work of the great geniuses tended to improve as they got older. This was the case with Goethe, Shakespeare, Beethoven, Michelangelo... In many instances, their supreme masterpiece was their final work, produced in extreme old age.

Co-author Tony Buzan was also becoming increasingly impressed, on his worldwide lecture tours, by the inquisitiveness and extreme readiness to learn of his older listeners. Again, this perception contradicted the currently accepted stereotype of the older person being resistant to new information and new techniques.

The Scientific and Mental Evidence on Ageing

The evidence we found, which is cited in this book, is most encouraging for our new view of ageing. Multiple evidence indicates that by using the brain well and properly as you get older, you physically change it, improving and streamlining its synaptic connections and hence its power of association. The autopsy on Einstein's brain after his death is a case in point. Einstein's brain revealed that it contained 400 per cent more glial cells than the norm. Since these cells specifically aid interconnectivity in the brain circuits, the effect would have been to boost his power of association, between apparently separate items, far beyond the average. Of course Einstein may have been exceptional in this respect, but it is an encouraging pointer for the rest of us.

The Benefits of Constant Challenge

We shall dispel the misconceptions that exist about the inevitable decline of the brain as age increases. It is popularly believed that one loses millions of brain cells every day through the attrition of encroaching age. This is simply not true. It is an ancient canard that has been passed around in circular fashion, with no substantive evidence whatsoever for it. We refute this harmful lie, citing proof from well-researched scientific sources. In fact, far from the brain cells dying off with age, their synaptic connections can be physically improved by proper exercise of the brain. Constant challenge and the solving of problems will physically improve your brain.

THE WISE

Previous human societies developed differing traditional and reverential names for the old, for example: patriarchs, matriarchs, oracles, the Wise, elders, sages and seers. In contrast, in modern society, the personality characteristics commonly attributed to the aged are stereotypical negatives, such as: obstinate, pig-headed, inflexible… How did this state of affairs come about? Such negative expressions are in fact simply a reversal of what should be seen as positive qualities. 'Stubborn' should, for instance, be re-interpreted as 'determined'. It is important to redefine the derogatory terms to reveal the positives that underlie them.

WAYS TO IMPROVE YOUR BRAIN

Naturally we recommend physical exercise with an aerobic element, as well as stressing the importance of a balanced diet and the harmful effects of smoking and excessive drinking. And, very importantly, we recommend mental exercise too. We advocate mind sports, teasers and puzzles, as brain callisthenics to stretch and challenge your mental powers. Memory and creativity techniques are studied, with a view to demonstrating how they can permit 50-somethings to compete with, and outwit, their younger rivals. On another level, current medical thinking indicates that Alzheimer's Disease may essentially be a rotting of inactive brains as they get older. We explore this and analyse whether there are possible defence systems, or even reversal methods — and what these might be.

Our programme consists of practical steps, with concrete examples. The aim is to encourage our readers to take renewed pride in themselves, and to challenge and stretch their imaginations, their creativity and, ultimately, their achievements. Readers will inevitably ask: How do I kick myself into action? Here we offer real, practical advice to make sure that your brains do not disintegrate!

AEROBIC EXERCISE AT HOME

Aerobic exercise is invaluable in increasing the efficiency with which oxygen is transported around the body. There are many forms of aerobic exercise, from a brisk walk with a dog to a strenuous game of squash, swimming, cycling, skipping and circuit training with weights.

In Chapters Seven and Eight we provide extensive guidelines for maintaining and improving your cardiovascular health.

MIND SPORTS

Having dealt with physical stimulation, and stressed the little-recognized fact that the brain is actually part of the body, we move on to the vital area of mental stimulation. One important branch of this comprises mind sports, brain-teasers and puzzles.

On 21 January 1995 the *Daily Telegraph* published an article stating that its readers were exhibiting an insatiable demand for items such as these, as expressed in their reader mailbag; accordingly, from that date it appointed a full-time Mind Games Editor and is now regularly devoting an entire page to the topic! Meanwhile, *The Times* now publishes bridge and chess articles every day, the latter written by co-author of *The Age Heresy*, chess Grand Master Ray Keene.

MEMORY

We also demonstrate memory systems that can be adapted to simple and effective everyday use. These include the 'memory theatre' and Tony Buzan's patent speciality, the colourful Mind Map, which helps you to remember complex formulas, lists, lecture material or notes for tests, exams or presentations. The Mind Map is fun and exciting, as well as extremely useful.

CREATIVITY

How can you increase your creativity? Most over-forties are widely expected to be suffering from a lessening of their creative drive. It is a commonplace of Academia that no worthwhile research in mathematics, for example, is done after the age of 26. In fact, most people are locked into a negative spiral regarding creativity, falsely

> ### BRAIN FLASH
>
> #### SYMBOLS OF INTELLIGENCE
> *Why are mind games, and chess in particular, so important to us? Throughout the history of culture, prowess at mind games has been associated with intelligence in general; and mind games do have an extraordinary pedigree. According to Dr Irving Finkel of the Western Asiatic Antiquities Department at the British Museum, game boards have been discovered in Palestine and Jordan dating back to Neolithic times, around 7,000 years BC. Astoundingly, this predates our current knowledge of when writing and pottery were introduced in those societies. Since many of the board games were found in tombs, it is likely that the shades of the departed had to play a game with the gods of the underworld to ensure safe conduct into the after-life.*
>
> *Board games are no longer regarded as a sort of IQ test for the dead, but they do retain their potency as symbols of intelligence.*

believing that the higher the number of ideas generated, the more the quality deteriorates – i.e., as quantity increases, quality decreases. In the course of this book we dramatically expose the widespread fallacies about declining creativity. Attendees at Tony Buzan's lectures have described his revelations on this topic as 'life-transforming'.

SMASHING THE AGE BARRIER

Current genetic thinking indicates that there is a maximum age-cap for human longevity, extending from the age of 85 to perhaps 125, at its outer limit. Citing the latest research, we explore whether this ultimate age barrier can be smashed. This is both a philosophical and a medical question of immense importance.

Sex

We look at the ageing brain in relation to sex, love and romance. Is it better at 70? We show that, if you stay fit and mentally alert, your sex life, far from declining with the years, will be a source of ever-increasing pleasure.

The Methuselah Mandate — the Golden Oldies

We look at the Great Oldies: notable examples of artists, leaders, mind sports champions and general achievers, whose work clearly improved with age, such as Shakespeare, Goethe, Beethoven, Brahms, Michelangelo… We spice our text with examples — quirky or fascinating — of extraordinary achievers, such as The Cricketer, Charles Absolon, who in the nineteenth century, between the ages of 60 and 90, took 8,500 wickets and scored 26,000 runs in first-class cricket. He captured 500 wickets in just one season, aged 57 (official figures taken from *Wisden*). And we look at amazing performances in mental sports and at the extraordinary records set in the Veterans' Olympics for Physical Sports.

Statistical Records

Statistics show the massive progress, the acceleration in speed, endurance, strength and flexibility, of older generations as time has gone by, and as they have put effort into their physical health on all levels.

Conclusion

Our central thrust is sensational and reverses conventional thinking! Your brain improves with age — if it is used well. We show how it has been done by others and how you, the reader, can do it for yourself.

Our revolutionary new thesis conforms, in fact, to a simple logic, if you think about it, which states that older people have experienced more — not less — than younger people and are therefore more adaptable, when retrained or forced to compete in brain power with younger generations.

STILL COMPETING!

Many people fear retirement, while simultaneously sensing that they have much to offer society in terms of their experience, which is being wasted. *The Age Heresy* explains clearly, succinctly and with the latest, convincing scientific evidence that **your thinking, creativity and general potential can increase with age, rather than evaporate.** Many of those with more free time on their hands still passionately believe that they have it in them to achieve dazzling levels of performance. And since 'jobs for life' no longer exist, the current trend proves the necessity to compete, even later in life. We show you how!

GLOBAL MEGA-TRENDS AND YOU

The baby-boom generation, born in the rush of enthusiasm just after the Second World War, was a generation born in hope, with – to borrow a phrase from that genius, Charles Dickens – 'Great Expectations'. The baby-boomers have been, and continue to be, a vast and trend-setting consumer group. In the year 1996, for example, someone hits the half-century mark every 17 seconds! Many of them are now wondering what the future holds, as they enter their forties and fifties. Governments worldwide, too, are wondering how best to utilize, care for and benefit from this generation. Will they become a drain on national and global economies – or a resource? Of the five billion people on this planet, soon over 50 per cent will be beyond the age of 50. And, sensationally, this group is predicted to corner 70 per cent of the world's wealth within the next decade.

The authors belong to this generation. We have been there, and still are there; we understand the problems and have devised our own specific solutions. We therefore speak with credibility about our own proposed solutions. We are not producing hypothetical agendas, we are preaching what we both practise!

WHAT SHOULD I DO NOW?

Read this book! From now on, at the end of each chapter, we give concrete advice and practical steps for your ongoing development. When bodily (and brain) functions decline, they can often be attributed to the following causes, in varying degrees:

1. inadequate exercise and an unhealthy diet
2. smoking and excessive drinking
3. conforming to expected patterns of behaviour (i.e., you behave as you think older people are meant to behave, rather than acting as you actually feel).

If all the above are addressed – and adjusted – by you, then you will be able to lead a more fulfilled life, and this book is going to tell you what you should, and should not, do to achieve this.

If you motivate yourself, strive for constant stimulation, and keep fit and healthy, you can be a superstar, too.

BRAIN FLASH

FINANCIAL MUSCLE
'Far from staying home to vegetate, Britain's over-fifties are getting out and about.

According to forecasts from the Henley Centre, by the year 2000 the number of people aged between 45 and 59 in the UK will increase by 11 per cent – to just under 9 million. The numbers are high because of the proportion of people now approaching middle age who were "baby-boomers" and born in the five years after the Second World War.

10 million people over the age of 50 in Britain take at least one holiday a year.
Freed from the burdens of supporting a family and paying a mortgage, many middle-aged and retired people have large amounts of disposable income and fewer financial responsibilities.

The over-fifties are "fitter and more adventurous" than previous generations, and even when in their seventies are not afraid to pursue active sports such as skiing. "People are retiring earlier and are healthier than ever before."'

CHAPTER ONE

GENESIS OF AN IDEA

—

'EDUCATION IS AN ORNAMENT IN PROSPERITY AND A REFUGE IN ADVERSITY. IT IS THE BEST PROVISION FOR OLD AGE. EDUCATED MEN AND WOMEN ARE AS MUCH SUPERIOR TO THE UNEDUCATED AS THE LIVING ARE TO THE DEAD.'

ARISTOTLE

INTRODUCTION

This chapter explains how the two co-authors, in different parts of the globe but at the same time, became fascinated by the question of why we are constantly being told that the brain packs up at the age of 26, whereas the people we were studying, the great geniuses, were obviously getting better and better with time. It is almost a mythical definition of how two people, at different places but at the same point in time, were drawn together to the same crossroads.

The statistical findings that we came across during our research indicated that the inherent potential of the brain, both atomically and anatomically, is infinitely greater than has generally been assumed. This leads to the inevitable conclusion that the potential for growth throughout a human lifetime has been systematically underestimated by a colossal margin. The hope contained in this information is one of the greatest omens for humankind as we approach the millennium and enter the twenty-first century.

THE HUMAN BRAIN AND ITS INTELLIGENCE

The genesis of this book can be traced to three particular moments in time, over a period of more than a decade, which 'met' and ignited, to create the flame of a new idea.

THE FIRST SPORE

The first moment was in May 1973, when Tony Buzan was International Editor of the magazine of Mensa, the society for those with a high IQ. He had been asked to process the information he had been gathering on the human brain and its intelligence, and to make suggestions based on that information. Here are his findings:

In all science disciplines – biochemistry, mathematics, physics, psychology and philosophy – researchers have found themselves drawn inevitably towards the same vortex: the brain-mind-body problem and the inherent question of the brain's potential. Meanwhile, fringe sciences, especially as the current millennium draws to a close, have been hurling some pretty hefty spanners into the traditional works.

It is now known, beyond doubt, that the mind is a fabric consisting of layers of interlinked networks, which can consciously control heartbeat, oxygen intake, internal organs and brain waves. Further, there is evidence to suggest that the mind has an even more extensive control over functions than was previously assumed.

In deep states of meditation or hypnosis, people have been observed to eliminate all pain, to paralyse a part of their body completely, to produce massive skin eruptions where no cause was apparent (and to eliminate them immediately afterwards), to induce any predetermined symptom artificially, to perform feats of strength normally attributed only to supermen or madmen, and to cure themselves of apparently incurable diseases.

In academic circles, researchers have performed experiments in retention and recall, which suggest that the basic storage capacity of the brain is absolute, in terms of remembering its own existence. Subjects whose brains were electronically probed produced complete, multisensory recall of situations randomly triggered and ranging over complete lifetimes. In addition, recent work on mnemonic systems indicates that, even without electric interference, the brain can remember a staggering 7,000 disconnected items. It can do this in sequence, in random order, and in reverse order, with no decline in performance as the number of items to be recalled is increased.

REASSESSMENT OF LEARNING

In view of this, it is now obvious that a complete reassessment of human learning and potential must be made. One of the first considerations is, of course, how best to educate an organ – the brain – that is estimated to possess virtually infinite possibilities for associative interconnecting. With such power available to us, it is apparent that our standard, inflexible, linear approaches are no longer acceptable.

It is equally apparent that standard psychological methods of testing ability must be totally changed, if not eliminated entirely. To judge an organ's capacity, for example, by its forced response to a question about shapes in an ink blot is ludicrous, when it is realized that the same organ can create multi-dimensional, holographic, varicoloured, original and projected images without assistance. This ability, variously labelled daydreaming, hallucinating or madness, is either taken for granted or denigrated. But it takes little acuity to realize that any organ that can both create and observe its own creation, at one and the same time, is spectacularly formidable.

Similarly, measuring general aptitude with standard 'intelligence quota'(IQ) tests is absurd. Rather than employing sterile tools which 'measure' whether some people are more 'interesting' and 'able' than others, surely it is time that we evolved. It is now the moment to see man, woman and the universe as they are: infinitely involved, infinitely fascinating and worthy, not of categorization and division, but of understanding.

THE SECOND SPORE

At exactly the same time that Tony Buzan was editing the international Mensa journal, and pondering on the significance of the information he had been gathering on the human brain, co-author Raymond Keene, at Trinity College, Cambridge, was studying European literature, language, history and culture, and specifically that towering German genius, Johann Wolfgang von Goethe.

Ray was struck by an apparently serious anomaly: he was constantly informed by members of the surrounding academic environment that the fires of creativity regularly 'burn out' by the age of 26. It was also commonly stated that chess players (and chess is Ray's second career) peak at 26 and then are 'past it'. 'Thinking like a 40-year-old' is, in fact, a common term of disparagement among chess players.

Such commonplaces of academic wisdom, though, did not sit well with the 'awkward' fact (one might say the glaring contradiction) that the work of the chess champions, artists, writers, trans-cultural giants, indeed of the inspirational greats and geniuses whom Ray was studying, frequently – rather than exceptionally – seemed to produce better work as they got older. Indeed, in many cases an artist's supreme creation, dwarfing all previous work, was his final piece, often brought to fruition in extreme old age.

All the great minds seemed to have a clear creative vision and purpose, and strove towards its fulfilment with barely credible levels of determination and persistence.

BEETHOVEN'S LAST

Should anyone doubt this, then simply examine the chronologically ordered numbers that define when a particular masterpiece was written or composed. Who would deny that Beethoven's Ninth Symphony (and he only wrote nine) marked his creative peak? Who would reject *Faust* Part II (and there are only two parts) as Goethe's deepest and richest work? And the list goes on... Shakespeare's late plays, in particular *The Tempest* (his last), are his most magical; Leonardo da Vinci started painting the Mona Lisa when he was 52; Michelangelo began work as papal architect-in-chief on St Peter's, in Rome, at the age of 63; Brahms's Fourth Symphony (he only wrote four) exceeds in its grandeur of structure and opulence of melody, its harmony and tonality, all his previous compositions. Brahms, in fact, only turned his hand to writing symphonies at all when he was 43 (Symphony No. I). Sinan, the imperial architect of the Istanbul of the Sultans, created his crowning glory, the Edirne Mosque, when in his eighties.

The answer had to be that some serious misconceptions were collectively, if subconsciously, developing. Academics were telling their students one thing, but were lecturing about works that refuted their own predictions. This phenomenon required both investigation and questioning.

THE THIRD SPORE

The third major event took place in April 1986, when an organization called the Turning Point asked Tony Buzan to address its monthly meeting in Stockholm. Turning Point had been formed by a group of minds who felt that humankind, and indeed the entire planet, was at a 'turning point'. Both as individuals and as a group, they needed to acquire as much information as possible to help them make a positive contribution to the future of the human race. During the course of his lecture on the brain Tony distributed a questionnaire. This asked the group's members to rate themselves on a scale of 0–100 in various categories, including learning skills, intelligence, general self-evaluation and hope for the future.

The average rating in each category was between 60 and 70. This was definitely above average, but far below what might be expected in a group that had come together specifically because it believed in the future and believed it could contribute to it.

As Tony continued to discuss the brain and the future, he was simultaneously exploring the question: 'What can one do to help individuals such as these (and indeed all individuals and groups), long past the stage of standard formal learning, to develop their phenomenal natural capacities in a way that is both continually self-regenerating and expansive?' Learning, thinking and self-improvement do not, of course (as is popularly supposed) cease when you leave school, college or university.

THE GOOD NEWS

As a result of these extraordinary confluences, the authors independently and together gathered data about what a human being *really* is, and what, therefore, its potential could be.

The Age Heresy is the answer for those who want to see their brains and mental performance continuously surge forward. **This book is for anyone who wishes to gain access to their brain and who simultaneously wishes to use it well for the whole of their life and at any age, from 8 to 80, and beyond!**

Research is increasingly proving that the creative and memory powers of the brain tend towards the infinite — and, far from declining, can actually increase as you age. We plan now to tell you how.

WHAT SHOULD I DO NOW?

First, read the next chapter to find out what your estimated life-expectancy is — then you can set about extending it, and maximizing the quality of time available to you.

BRAIN FLASH

ON THE BRAIN BEAT

'No superlative, it seems, is too grand to explain what is happening to brain research, precisely midway through the international "Decade of the Brain". Gerald Fischback, Professor of Neurobiology at Harvard, believes philosophers enquiring into the human condition can no longer ignore the brain experiments that are "among the most urgent, challenging and exciting" in all of science. "Our survival, and probably the survival of this planet, depends on a more complete understanding of the human mind," he says.

The brain weighs about the same as a bag of sugar — about 2 per cent of body weight — but accounts for up to 20 per cent of the body's energy needs.

A million million nerve cells are packed into every human head. There are as many stars in the Milky Way galaxy as there are cells between your ears.

Each nerve cell can be connected with up to 100,000 others. Counting each nerve connection in the human brain cortex — the outer layer — at the rate of one a second would take 32 million years.

As each connection involves at least 50 different chemical transmitters, **the human brain is the most complex structure known to the human mind.**

Plato, the Greek philosopher who was born in 428 BC, was the first to conclude, correctly, that the brain was the "originating power of the perceptions and hearing and sight and smell".'

CHAPTER TWO

THE LONGEVITY EVERESTS

'AND NOW, LEST HE PUT FORTH HIS HAND, AND TAKE ALSO OF THE TREE OF LIFE, AND EAT, AND LIVE FOR EVER. THEREFORE THE LORD GOD SENT HIM FORTH FROM THE GARDEN OF EDEN... AND THE LORD SAID, MY SPIRIT SHALL NOT ALWAYS STRIVE WITH MAN, FOR THAT HE ALSO IS FLESH: YET HIS DAYS SHALL BE AN HUNDRED AND TWENTY YEARS.'

THE BOOK OF GENESIS

INTRODUCTION

This chapter is a call to arms and a challenge to prevailing misconceptions about age. You will be introduced to the extraordinary realities of what has been achieved in terms of human longevity. And we provide a bench-mark test that allows you to calculate your own predicted life-expectancy and shows you how to adjust it appropriately – down or up!

FAMILY TREE

The generational longevity record has, fascinatingly, been achieved over 2,700 unbroken years by the family of the celebrated Chinese philosopher K'ung Fu-tzu, otherwise, and more famously, known as Confucius.

The lineage of Confucius (551–479 BC) can be traced back further than that of any other family. His great-, great-, great-, great-grandfather K'ung Chia is known from the eighth century BC, while Confucius's 85th direct lineal descendants, Wei-yi (b. 1939) and Wei-ning (b. 1947) are alive today in Taiwan.

INDIVIDUAL LONGEVITY

The latest census in China revealed 3,800 centenarians, of whom two-thirds were women. In the USA, in January 1996, the figure was 50,000, having risen by 13,000 in the previous five years. By the year 2050 there will be 1.2 million American centenarians – 0.3 per cent of the overall US population.

THE OLDEST AUTHENTIC CENTENARIAN

The greatest authenticated age to which any human had ever lived was 120 years 237 days, in the case of Shigechiyo Izumi of Asan on Tokunoshima, an island south-west of Tokyo. He was born at Asan on 29 June 1865 and was recorded as a 6-year-old in Japan's first census of 1871. He died at 12.15 GMT on 21 February 1986 after developing pneumonia. He worked until he was 105. He attributed his long life to 'God, Buddha and the Sun'. But on 21 February 1996 the amazing Jeanne Calment celebrated her 121st birthday!

OLDEST PERSON EVER

The oldest person in the world, whose date of birth can be reliably authenticated, is now Jeanne Louise Calment, who was born in France on 21 February 1875. She lives in a nursing home in Arles, southern France, where she cele-

---

BRAIN FLASH

OLDEST OLD, NOT BABY-BOOMERS, ARE THE FASTEST-GROWING AGE GROUP

'The fastest-growing segment of the US population is not the middle-aged – the baby boomers – or the merely old, but the oldest old, the people who are 85 and older.

The oldest old remain a tiny percentage of the US population overall, but their numbers are climbing faster than those of any other age group. In the last 35 years, the population of 85-plusers increased by 232 per cent, compared with an expansion of 30 per cent for the population as a whole. Right now, the oldest old account for 1.2 per cent of the population, but by some projections that figure could rise to nearly 10 per cent by the middle of the next century.

At first thought, this ripening of America offers an image of inexorably increasing decrepitude – and an ever more unbearable medical bill for younger generations.

But gerontologists say that people in their nineties and above may in fact be a healthier group overall than people 20 years their junior.'

THE TOP TEN: AUTHENTIC NATIONAL LONGEVITY RECORDS					
COUNTRY	YEARS	DAYS	NAME	BORN	DIED
1. FRANCE	121	+	JEANNE LOUISE CALMENT	21 FEB 1875	FL.MAR 1996
2. JAPAN	120	237	SHIGECHIYO IZUMI	29 JUN 1865	21 FEB 1986
3. UK	118	+	CHARLOTTE HUGHES	1 AUG 1877	FL.JAN 1996
4. USA	116	88	CARRIE WHITE	18 NOV 1874	14 FEB 1991
5. CANADA	113	124	PIERRE JOUBERT	15 JUL 1701	16 NOV 1814
6. AUSTRALIA	112	330	CAROLINE MAUD MOCKRIDGE	11 DEC 1874	6 NOV 1987
7. SPAIN	112	228	JOSEFA SALAS MATEO	14 JUL 1860	27 FEB 1973
8. NORWAY	112	61	MAREN BOLETTE TORP	21 DEC 1876	20 FEB 1989
9. MOROCCO	112	+	EL HADJ MOHAMMED EL MOKRI	1844	16 SEP 1957
10. POLAND	112	+	ROSWLIA MIELCZARAK	1868	7 JAN 1981

FL = FLOURISHING (I.E., STILL ALIVE)

It should be noted that the respected international journal TIME, (issue March 18 1996), pressed the claims of Brazilian Maria Do Carmo Geronimo as being 125, with a valid birth certifiate. The world-wide prominence given to Jeanne Calment may well lead to further claims of this type which will need careful scrutiny before verification.

brated her 121st birthday in 1996 with champagne. She once met Vincent Van Gogh (who died on 29 July 1890) in her father's shop.

AMAZING AGE FACTS

Human beings are not the only living things with astonishing longevity records. **The oldest continuously living things in the world are plants. One specimen of the Californian creosote plant is 11,700 years old.**

The oldest living tree in the world is a Californian bristlecone pine named 'Methuselah', which is 4,700 years old, and still going strong! This tree was alive when Homer composed the *Iliad*, when Buddha preached Nirvana, and when Christ gave the Sermon on the Mount.

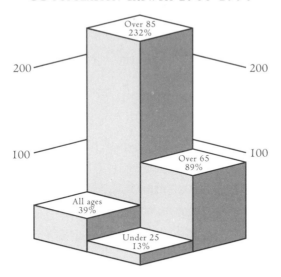

US POPULATION GROWTH 1960-1990

Corroborative evidence of US population growth comes from a chart published in the respected US journal Time Magazine.

The oldest *revived* living entities in the world are bacterial spores, lying dormant inside a fossil bee, which suddenly surged back to life, after 40 million years. This feat of resurrection was achieved by microbiologists Raul Cano and Monica Borucki of the California Polytechnic State University. Their work was carried out in early 1995 and involved releasing small stingless bees from fossilized tree sap or amber.

THE LONG-LIFE QUIZ: CHECK YOUR OWN LIFE-EXPECTANCY

Dr Diana Woodruff is a psychologist who believes that we all have the capacity to live to be 100. In fact, as we mention at the start of this chapter, biologists now set the upper limit for human life even higher – maybe as high as 125. Indeed, they are in excellent company. Although the biblically sanctioned life-span is normally said to be 'three score years and ten' (= 70), the Book of Genesis mentions that man's days 'shall be an hundred and twenty

S. Markewitz/Telegraph Colour Library

ABOVE: The over-fifties are 'fitter and more adventurous' than previous generations and are not afraid to pursue active sports such as skiing.

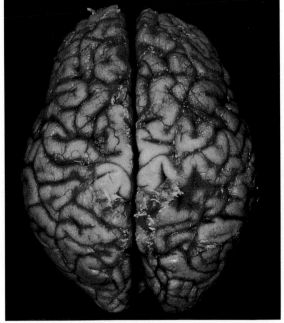

RIGHT: The left and right hemispheres of the brain deal with different intellectual functions but must be used together.

Dr. Colin Chumbley/Science Photo Library

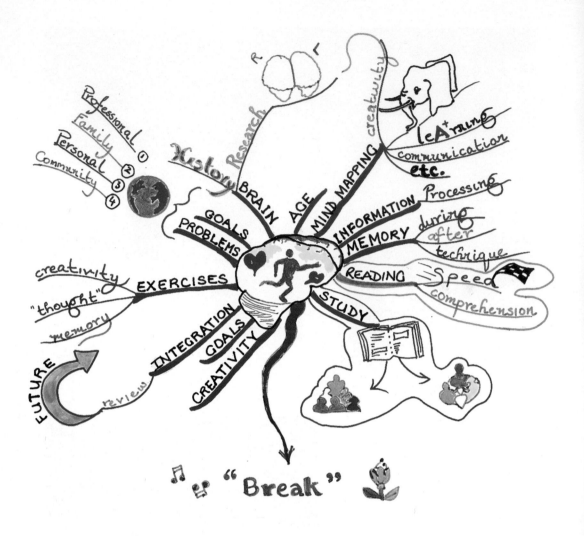

Re-formatted by Lady Mary Tovey

ABOVE: This Mind Map depicts a complete mind and body course on improving with age. The central image is a brain, linked with the physical body, and two hearts, representing emotional and cardiovascular health.

BASIC LIFE-EXPECTANCY CHART

PRES. AGE	EST. LIFE EXPEC.	PRES. AGE	EST. LIFE EXPEC.	PRES. AGE	EST. LIFE EXPEC.	PRES. AGE	EST. LIFE EXPEC.	PRES. AGE	EST. LIFE EXPEC.
15	70.7	29	71.7	43	72.8	57	75.4	71	80.7
16	70.8	30	71.8	44	72.9	58	75.5	72	81.2
17	70.8	31	71.8	45	73.0	59	76.0	73	81.7
18	70.8	32	71.9	46	73.2	60	76.3	74	82.2
19	70.9	33	72.0	47	73.3	61	76.6	75	82.8
20	71.1	34	72.0	48	73.5	62	77.0	76	83.3
21	71.1	35	72.1	49	73.6	63	77.3	77	83.9
22	71.2	36	72.2	50	73.8	64	77.7	78	84.5
23	71.3	37	72.2	51	74.0	65	78.1	79	85.1
24	71.3	38	72.3	52	74.2	66	78.4	80	85.7
25	71.4	39	72.4	53	74.4	67	78.9	81	86.3
26	71.5	40	72.5	54	74.7	68	79.3	82	87
27	71.6	41	72.6	55	74.9	69	79.7	83	87.6
28	71.6	42	72.7	56	75.1	70	80.2	84	88.2

years'. After years of research on longevity we have drawn up the quiz that follows, which enables you to work out how long you will live. Our own view is that intellectually and physically active, contented fun-lovers have the best chance of living to be 100 or more.

Start by looking up your present age in the table. Against this, you will find your basic life-expectancy, derived from figures produced by insurance actuaries. Then, in answering the questions on the following pages, add to or take away from this figure, according to how your own lifestyle and personality affect your habits.

Remember one thing: women can expect to live roughly three years longer than men (on whom the above table is based). Women should therefore add three years to their basic life-expectancy.

How to Calculate Your Own Life-Expectancy

1. Add one year for each of your grandparents who lived to be 80 or more, or is 80 and still alive. Add half a year for each one who topped 70, or is 70 and still alive.

2. Add four years if your mother lived beyond 80, and two years if your father did as well. Do the same for living parents who have reached these ages.

3. Take off four years if any sister, brother, parent or grandparent died of a heart attack, stroke or arteriosclerosis before the age of 50. Subtract two years for each of these who died between 50 and 60.

4. Take off three years for each sister, brother, parent or grandparent who died of *diabetes mellitus* or peptic ulcer before 60. If any of these died of stomach cancer before then, subtract two years. For any other illnesses that killed them before 60 (except those caused by accidents) subtract one year.

5. Women who cannot have children, or plan none, subtract half a year. Women with over seven children take off one year.

6. If you are a first-born, add one year.

7. Add two years if your intelligence is above average (i.e., if you have an IQ of over 100).

8. Smoking: take off 12 years (yes, 12) if you smoke more than 40 cigarettes a day; if 20–40 cigarettes, subtract seven years; but if you smoke fewer than 20 per day, subtract two years.

9. If you enjoy regular sex once or twice a week, add two years.

10. If you have an annual check-up (a thorough one), add two years.

11. If you are overweight (or ever have been), take off two years.

12. If you sleep more than 10 hours every night, or less than 5 hours a night, take off two years.

13. Drinking: one or two whiskies, or one pint/half a litre of wine, or up to a maximum of four glasses of beer per day, counts as moderate – add three years. If you don't drink every day – add only one and a half years. If you don't drink at all, don't add or subtract anything. Heavy drinkers and alcoholics – take off eight years.

14. Exercise: three times a week — jogging, cycling, swimming, brisk walks, dancing, skating, etc. — add three years. Weekend walks don't count.

15. Do you prefer simple, plain foods, vegetables and fruit to richer, meatier, fatty foods? If you can say yes honestly, and stop eating before you are full, add one year.

16. If you are frequently ill, take off five years.

17. Education: if you did postgraduate work at university, add three years. For an ordinary bachelor's degree, add two. Up to A-level, add one. O-level and below — none.

18. Jobs: if you are a professional person, add one and a half years; technical, managerial, administrative and agricultural workers, add one year; proprietors, clerks and sales staff, add nothing; semi-skilled workers, take off half a year; labourers, subtract four years.

19. If, however, you're not a labourer but your job involves a lot of physical work, add two years. If it is a desk job, take off two years.

20. If you live in a town, or have done for most of your life, take off one year. Add a year if most of your time has been spent in the countryside.

21. If you are married and living with your spouse, add one year. However, if you are a separated man living alone, take off nine years; seven if you are a widower living alone. If you live with others, take off only half these figures. Women who are separated or divorced, take off four years; widows, three and a half, unless you live with others, in which case take off only two.

22. If you have one or two close friends in whom you confide, add a year.

23. Add two years if you regularly play mind sports.

24. If your attitude to life is both positive and realistic, add four years.

Armed with this information you can now calculate your own life-expectancy. Remember to add three years if you are female.

The results of this quiz are a guide to your probable life-expectancy if you continue your patterns of behaviour as they are at present. The remainder of *The Age Heresy* is designed to encourage you to increase your score (no matter what it is now) dramatically.

WHAT SHOULD I DO NOW?

1. If you smoke, first cut down, then give up the habit entirely (see in particular Chapter Four).

2. Have a thorough annual medical check-up.

3. If you are over- or underweight, find the appropriate weight for you as an individual and work towards achieving it. Ask your doctor what your ideal weight should be.

4. If you drink heavily, cut down.

5. Take up regular exercise, particularly aerobic exercise, and aim to do this for at least 20 minutes thrice-weekly.

6. Take up mind sports, such as chess, bridge or 'Go'.

You may think that you can't do all, or indeed any, of the above, but in Chapter Four we will show you how!

BRAIN FLASH

THE DRINK TANK
'Wine is the most healthful and hygienic of beverages.'
Louis Pasteur, French scientist

'Drink no longer water but use a little wine for thy stomach's sake and thine other infirmities.'
The Bible, Timothy I

'There are more old drunkards than old doctors.'
Benjamin Franklin, US scientist and statesman

'Red wine can be a part of your regular diet, as long as you do not drink excessively — no more than about half a litre a day.'
Michel Montignac, French dietician and bestselling author

Chapter Three

Manufacturing Your Own Time?

'Had we but world enough and time.'

Andrew Marvell, 'To His Coy Mistress'

Introduction

In this chapter we look at two different ways of staying vigorous and fit, and of extending your life-expectancy – in other words, 'manufacturing your own time'. The first is what might be termed the new snake-oil (HRT or Hormone Replacement Therapy). Is it a good thing? Somehow we doubt it. Instead, we recommend drawing on your own physical and mental resources to stay young and fit. And we list the top 20 areas of mental performance that require improvement among 40–50-year-olds and begin to show you how to achieve this. For the more you learn, the easier it becomes to learn more.

Stopping the Clock

'You can be as vibrant at 60 as you were at 30!'

How often have you heard this claim, offering the elixir of eternal youthfulness? It is made increasingly by the purveyors of Human Growth Hormones, who assert that the demonstrable benefits, to both men and women, of taking such substances include: higher energy levels; increased stamina; greater sex drive; retrieval of former quality of skin elasticity, normally associated with younger people; stronger bones; and more efficiently functioning hearts. Courses of testosterone, to cope with the male andropause, and of oestrogen, to combat the female menopause, are the favoured methods by those who

> ### BRAIN FLASH
>
> #### 100 GOING ON 45!
>
> *Edward L. Bernays coined the term 'public relations' in 1919 and is widely recognized as the father of public relations. When he turned 100 he said his mental age was 'no different from when I was 45'. He added: 'When you reach 100 don't let it throw you, because a person has many ages, and chronological is the least important.'*

choose to use them — and some claim the effect is miraculous. Others accuse the purveyors of being nothing better than 'snake-oil salesmen', who are cynically 'medicalizing' the normal ageing process.

For example, *Time Magazine* wrote on 26 June 1995:

'Oestrogen is indeed the closest thing in modern medicine to an elixir of youth — a drug that slows the ravages of time for women. It is already the No.1 prescription drug in America, and it is about to hit its demographic sweet spot: the millions of baby-boomers, now experiencing their first hot flushes… but what today's women should know is that, like every other magic potion, this one has a dark side.

'To gain the full benefits of oestrogen, a woman must take it not only at menopause, but also for decades afterward. It means a life-time of drug-taking and possible side-effects that include an increased risk of several forms of cancer… weighing such risks against the truly miraculous benefits of oestrogen may be the most difficult health decision a woman can make.'

Whether to take HRT in the form of oestrogen or testosterone is clearly a matter for individual choice.

SELF-RELIANCE STRATEGY

What we offer here is quite different. Our own strategy, as mapped out in this book, is one that allows the reader to draw entirely on his or her untapped inner resources and strength. We do recommend a healthy diet and vitamins, not drugs, as well as aerobic exercise, but the main thrust of our argument is to show you how your mental performance can improve with age, simply by harnessing the phenomenal power within your own personal bio-computer and by learning the truth about what can actually happen to your brain as you age.

CONSIDER THIS

Your brain is a sleeping giant. Many experts believe that we use as little as I per cent of our full potential.

Even though you have probably spent between I,000 and I0,000 hours formally learning history, languages, literature, mathematics, geography and political science… you will probably, no matter *what* age you are now, have spent only a few hours specifically learning the following skills:

- ☆ Creative thinking
- ☆ Concentration – memory performance
- ☆ The relationship between brain function and ageing
- ☆ The art of communication
- ☆ Comprehensive approaches to study and technical reading
- ☆ The effect of our modes of thought on habit patterns and change (meta-positive thinking).

CONCENTRATION AND COMPREHENSION

Statistics show that, on average, executives, businessmen and -women, academics and all professionals spend:

- ☆ 30 per cent of their professional time reading and sorting through information
- ☆ 20 per cent of their time solving problems and thinking creatively
- ☆ 20 per cent of their time communicating.

It is therefore essential that these skills be learnt by *everyone* and that the brain be trained accordingly.

BENEFITS

The strategy outlined in this book will give you the techniques and the knowledge to become more effective, and a much better thinker and communicator, as you progress through life. You will be able to:

☆ Remember names, facts and figures using memory techniques that are easy to learn and master.

☆ Achieve higher levels of creativity, clearer organization of your thoughts, increased concentration and more concise communications through the introduction and use of Mind Mapping. This is a technique for accessing your range of intelligence, improving all your thinking skills and dramatically improving your memory and creativity.

☆ Read more rapidly and assimilate all the materials you need to.

☆ Gain greater insights into your own potential by learning from the principles and techniques used by great minds in the business, sport and creative worlds. You will be shown ways of applying these principles in order to improve your own potential for greater success.

With this knowledge you will be able to achieve just about anything you set out to achieve, and do it progressively better as you mature!

LEARNING HOW TO LEARN AT ANY AGE

The Age Heresy is designed to assist you in the next leap in evolution: the awareness of intelligence by itself, and the knowledge that this intelligence too can be nurtured, starting at any time, and at any age, to astounding advantage. Consider the following:

INTELLECTUAL CAPITAL

✰ Stock-market analysts watch, like hawks, 10 individuals in Silicon Valley, California. When there is even a hint that one of them might move from Company A to Company B, the world's stock markets shift.

✰ The Manpower Services Commission in England publishes a survey in which it is noted that of the top 10 per cent of British companies, 80 per cent invest considerable money and time in training. In the bottom 10 per cent, no money or time is invested in training.

✰ In Minnesota, the Plato computer education project raises the thinking and academic performance levels of 20,000 pupils.

✰ In the armed forces of an increasing number of countries, mental martial arts have become as important as physical combat skills.

✰ National Olympic squads devote as much as 30 per cent of their training time to the development of mind-set, stamina and visualization skills.

✰ In the Fortune 500 (the 500 most successful companies defined annually by *Fortune* magazine), the top five computer companies alone spend more than a billion dollars on educating their employees.

✰ In Caracas, Dr Luis Alberto Machado became the first human being to be given a government portfolio as Minister of Intelligence, with a political mandate to raise the level of the mental power of an entire nation.

✰ The brain and intelligence have become the No.1 cover story in magazines and journals around the world.

Let us now consider this encouraging news in a different context. Many people in their forties and fifties are anxious to improve their mental performance and powers, but are still facing difficulty in achieving their goals.

The following pages take you on a quick guided tour of the problems that people increasingly face as they get older. These are the main areas we suggest you consider as the basis for the developing your own intellectual capital as you age. Many of the themes touched upon here will be developed and expanded in later chapters.

Over the past 20 years we have polled more than 100,000 people on each of the five continents. Among the more than 100 mental skill areas commonly mentioned as requiring improvement, here are the top 20:

THE TOP 20 AREAS OF MENTAL PERFORMANCE REQUIRING IMPROVEMENT AMONG 40–50-YEAR-OLDS

1. Memory
2. Concentration
3. Presentation skills/public speaking
4. Presentation skills/written
5. Creative thinking
6. Planning
7. Thought organization
8. Problem-analysis
9. Problem-solving
10. Motivation
11. Analytical thinking
12. Prioritizing
13. Reading speed (volume of material)
14. Reading comprehension
15. Time management
16. Stress
17. Fatigue
18. Assimilation of information
19. Getting started at all (i.e., procrastination or time-wasting) – and, of course, last but definitely not least, as you would expect…
20. Decline of mental ability with age.

With the aid of modern research into the functioning of the brain, each of these areas can be tackled with relative ease. We shall now touch on seven major topics that impinge on all of the above problems:

1. Left and right brain research
2. Mind Mapping ™
3. Speed-reading
4. Mnemonic techniques
5. Memory loss after learning
6. The brain cell – and, most importantly, …
7. 'Decline' of mental abilities with age.

We shall relate each of these topics to the major problem areas and we shall show how your new knowledge can be applied to the general improvement of mental performance.

I. LEFT AND RIGHT BRAIN RESEARCH

It has now become common knowledge that the left and right hemispheres of the brain deal with different intellectual functions. The left cortex primarily handles logic, language, number, sequence, analysis and listing; the right deals with rhythm, dimension, colour, imagination, daydreaming and spatial relationships.

What has only recently been realized is that the left cortex is not the so-called academic side, nor is the right cortex the so-called creative, intuitive, emotional side. We now know, from extensive research, that the two hemispheres need to be used in conjunction for there to be both academic and creative success.

The Einsteins, Newtons, Goethes and Shakespeares of this world, like the great business geniuses, combined their linguistic, numerical and analytical skills with their powers of imagination, in order to produce their creative masterpieces.

Using this basic knowledge of our brain's functioning, it is possible to train ourselves in skills relating to each of the problem areas, often producing incremental improvements of as much as 500 per cent.

Tony Buzan's key contribution to achieving such improvement is the Mind Map.

2. MIND MAPPING

In traditional note-taking — whether it be for memory, for the preparation of communication, for the organization of thought, for problem-analysis, for planning or for creative thinking — the standard mode of depiction is black and white, linear: sentences, short phrase lists, or numerically and alphabetically ordered lists. These methods, because of their lack of colour, visual rhythm, dimensions, images and spatial relationships, cauterize the brain's thinking capacities and are literally counter-productive to each of the aforementioned processes.

Mind Mapping (see Chapter Nine for further details) uses the full range of your brain's abilities, placing a colourful image in the centre of the page to facilitate memorization and the creative generation of ideas, and subsequently branching out in associative networks that mirror externally the brain's internal structures. The Mind Map can encapsulate a mass of information within a very small space, and can be used for both previewing and reviewing purposes.

By using Mind Maps, the preparation of speeches can be reduced in time terms from days to minutes; problems can be solved more rapidly; memory can be improved from failing to perfect; and creative thinkers can generate a limitless number of ideas rather than a short list. This is especially valuable if you feel that your memory and mental faculties are fading with age. The Mind Map is the perfect antidote.

3. SPEED-READING

It is possible to combine Mind Mapping with the new speed-reading techniques, which reach speeds of more than 1,000 words a minute. This can be achieved in conjunction with excellent comprehension, and the faster you can assimilate information, the more you can stimulate your brain and expand your horizons. Individuals, especially in companies, who can train themselves to do this, can them form Intellectual Commando Units, as described below.

Speed-reading may sound difficult and esoteric, but it is quite easy to start. Try this simple test, for instance. Time yourself reading a page of this book. Now read another page and time yourself again, but also do the following:

1. Use a pointer to help you focus. You were possibly told not to do this at school. If so, they were wrong!
2. Follow your pointer and only go forwards. Do not backslide or re-read segments.
3. Take in two words at a time, where before you took in one. This simple exercise will probably double your reading speed.

FORMING INTELLECTUAL COMMANDO UNITS

Reading at more advanced speeds, Mind Mapping in detail the outline of a book and its chapters, and exchanging the information gathered by using advanced Mind Mapping and presentation skills, it is possible for an individual to acquire, integrate, memorize and begin to apply in their professional situation an entire book's worth of new information in just one day. The implications for a company, of a number of its employees doing likewise simultaneously, are obvious.

4. MNEMONIC TECHNIQUES

Mnemonics is the art of assisting memory, using a device such as a rhyme to achieve this – for example, 'Thirty days hath September, April, June and November' to remember the number of days in the months. Mnemonic techniques were invented by the Greeks, and were, until quite recently, dismissed as 'tricks'. We now realize that these devices are soundly based on the brain's functioning, and that, when applied appropriately, they can dramatically improve memory performance.

Mnemonics uses the principles of association, and imagination, making dramatic, colourful, sensual and consequently unforgettable images in your mind. The Mind Map is, in fact, a superb multi-dimensional mnemonic, using the brain's innate functional areas effectively to imprint the required information upon itself. You can start by remembering the people you meet at parties, by associating their names with something distinctive about their appearance.

Using mnemonics, businessmen and -women have been trained to remember perfectly 40 newly introduced people, and to memorize lists of over 100 products, facts and data. These techniques are now being applied at the IBM training centre in Stockholm, and have been a major reason for the success of its introductory training programme.

5. MEMORY LOSS AFTER LEARNING AND WITH AGEING

This is a dramatic problem. After a one-hour learning period, there is a short rise in the recall of information as the brain integrates the new data. This is followed by a dramatic decline. By the end of 24 hours, as much as 80 per cent of the detail has been lost.

This loss is often confused by the 'loser' with the decline of mental abilities with *age*. The truth of the matter is that the loss of recall ability is entirely, and only, due to standard recall curves. It should in no way be confused with age. With appropriate training, as we shall indicate, memory can actually improve with age.

The implications of these facts and misconceptions are disturbing, especially for business. If a multinational firm spends $50 million a year on training, within a few days of that training's completion — if there is not an appropriate review programmed into the educational structure — the value of $40 million worth of training will have been lost. However, by understanding the memory's rhythms it is possible to avert this loss.

6. THE BRAIN CELL

In the last five years the brain cell has become the new frontier in the human search for knowledge. We have discovered that not only do we each have 1,000,000,000,000 (one billion) brain cells, but that the interconnections between them can form patterns and memory traces that combine to give a number so staggeringly large as to be functionally equivalent to infinite. The number, calculated by the Russian neuroanatomist, Pyotr Anokhin, is 1 followed by 6 ½ million miles (10.5 million km) of standard (11pt) typewritten noughts.

Your brain, in just one second, can grasp concepts that it would take a mainframe Cray super-computer, operating at 400 million calculations per second, 100 years to accomplish. It is clear that we have an inherent capacity to integrate and juggle with multiple billions of bits of data. It has, therefore, become increasingly apparent to those involved in brain research that adequate training of the phenomenal bio-computer that each of us possesses will enormously accelerate and increase our ability to problem-solve, to prioritize, to create and to communicate.

And training or, to put it more excitingly, challenging and stimulating the brain is not solely the prerogative of 'young trainees'. You can start at any age. The more you learn, the easier it is to learn more and the more your brain builds both mental and physical associational networks, making it increasingly easy to access and manipulate data.

7. 'DECLINE' OF MENTAL ABILITIES WITH AGE

The usual response to the question: 'What happens to your brain cells as they get older?' is: 'They die.' But one of the most delightful pieces of news from the brain-research front comes from Dr Marion Diamond of the University of California, who has recently confirmed that there is *no* brain-cell loss with age, in normal, active and healthy brains. On the contrary, research is now indicating that if the brain is used and trained, there is an *increase* in the brain's interconnective complexity — that is, intelligence is raised.

THE INTELLIGENCE REVOLUTION

We are at the beginning of a revolution, the like of which the world has never seen before: a huge leap in the development of human intelligence. In education, in business, and on the personal front, information from the psychological, neurophysiological and educational laboratories is being mobilized to dispel problems that had hitherto been accepted as part of the human ageing process.

By applying our knowledge of the brain's separate functions, by externally representing our internal mental processes in Mind Map form, by making use of the innate elements and rhythms of memory, and by applying our new-found knowledge of the brain cell and the possibilities for continued improvement throughout our lives, we come to realize that a massive leap in evolution is not only possible, but is in the process of happening. This book is in the vanguard.

Welcome, then, to the next great human adventure. An adventure in the exploration of your own and other people's vast and growing intelligences

– intelligences that should be expanding throughout life; an adventure that will prove stimulating, challenging and profound. That adventure is you.

WHAT SHOULD I DO NOW?

1. Remember this most important fact: the more you learn, the easier it is to learn more!

2. Learn how to speed-read – using the tips given in this chapter. If you read at a faster rate, you can acquire information more readily and expand your horizons.

3. Try to improve your memory. Start with the names of people you meet at parties. Look for something distinctive in their appearance or at what they are wearing – so that you can lock their name onto it. Use mnemonic techniques to help you remember the names.

4. Look at questions and problems from all sides. **Think flexible.** Try new solutions and experiences, as these will help you retain your mental alertness.

5. Become socially involved. It is an established fact that degeneration occurs faster among older people who withdraw from an active social life. Meet people. Try to solve their problems!

BRAIN FLASH

Sinan (1491–1588)

Sinan, the imperial architect of Sultan Suleiman the Magnificent, was first appointed to his job at the age of 47. During his remaining 50 years he designed and completed no fewer than 500 buildings, including palaces, tombs, hospitals, schools and public baths, as well as the greatest mosques in the Ottoman Empire. Sinan saw the dimensions and architectural brilliance of the Christian church Hagia Sophia in Istanbul (like the Parthenon in Athens, a monument to 'Divine Intelligence') as his lifelong challenge. He finally achieved his ambition to equal its beauty and surpass its size in his eighties, with the completion of his Selimiye Mosque at Edirne. He wrote proudly in his (even later) memoirs: 'Christians say that they have defeated the Muslims, because no dome has been built in the Islamic world which can rival the dome of Hagia Sophia. I determined to create such a dome.'

CHAPTER FOUR

THE METHUSELAH MANDATE

———

'MISS NOT THE DISCOURSE OF THE ELDERS.'
ECCLESIASTES, 8:9

INTRODUCTION

We have discovered in previous chapters that there are indeed tools and methodologies for improving your various intelligences. In this chapter we take you to the core of our entire argument. We reveal the ultimate good news – that your brain is a flexible, organic, constantly changing and, hopefully, constantly growing organ. As we progress through life it can (and *will* if you apply the messages of this book) continue to become increasingly complex, more sophisticated, more elegant and more useful to its owner.

Your ability to transform harmful habits and attitudes to take on new modes of behaviour is vital to improved performance as you age. It's never too late to start, and *now* is the time to begin. Prepare for some news about yourself that ranks in importance with Einstein's discovery of how to split the atom.

THE METHUSELAH MANDATE, THE BRAIN CELL AND 'META-POSITIVE THINKING' – THE POWER TO CHANGE YOURSELF FOR THE BETTER

In the pages that follow we shall discuss a subject of increasing global interest and importance. **That is: what actually happens to the human brain, as it progresses through the decades of its existence.** We will supply evidence for the case we are making: that, with appropriate training, most of the standard

41

'delusions' about the brain can be laid to rest and a new awareness of what actually does happen can be initiated – a complete revolution in learning, if you will.

Methuselah was, of course, according to the Bible, the oldest known human (in Genesis it is said that he lived for 969 years), and 'The Methuselah Mandate' is a call for all humans to achieve the full realization of their potential throughout life.

As individuals you, our readers, have become, perhaps without realizing it, the biggest star on the planet! After film stars, music and rock stars, now a new star is rising rapidly in the intellectual firmament – and that star is you. The human race is beginning to discover itself.

It is interesting to study memory, the brain cell, creativity and so on, but arguably the most fascinating topic is to study all those in the context of their progression through life. What we would like to do, first of all, is show you the standard graph depicting what is supposed to happen to the brain as it gets older.

The vertical axis represents intellectual capacity – or skills – and the horizontal axis represents time. Standard graphs on intelligence published by

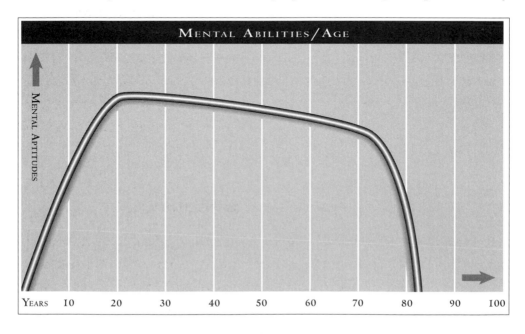

psychologists such as Hans Eysenck (you will find these in most introductory psychological texts) show that there is a phenomenal early growth in intellectual skills. This reaches a peak between the late teens and early twenties. Researchers usually go on to cite vast amounts of evidence to support this, including stories about the great mathematicians and how, throughout history, without exception, they have never done any great original work after the age of 26.

IQ tests generally confirm this, and studies by people reporting on themselves show that they think their memories are definitely deteriorating with age. In other words, their experience of their own mental process, as they age, is a reductionist and diminishing one.

THE MARTIAN PERSPECTIVE — WAR OF THE WORLDS

There is also the physical correlation that, after the age of 26, all the body's physical skills tend to decline. The obvious assumption is therefore that, as the physical body is declining, and as brain cells are part of that physical body, so they are obviously deteriorating as well. There is then a steady process of degeneration, with a rapid decline near the end. A very happy picture!

It is worth thinking about this. Take a Martian perspective, and say that, as Martians, we don't particularly like that bunch of animals down there on planet Earth, so what's a good way to de-motivate them (de-motive-atc, meaning to take away the life force)? One way, we might suggest, would be to send down a message to everybody saying, 'By the way, if you are over 26 you are disintegrating. Have a nice day!'

THE DELIGHTS OF DISINTEGRATION

What happens to your brain cells every day? Most people relate that they die, they drop off, they disintegrate, they disassociate from each other. We have asked people in every single country we have visited. On every single continent of the world, over a time period of more than 20 years, the answer has always been the same – in England, in New Mexico, in Taiwan, in Argentina, always the same reply: 'They die!' Every group of people 'knows' this information. What impact do you think this has on the planet? And when we ask how many brain cells die each day, again the reply comes with certainty, and almost with a sense of delight: *about a million*.

Now, imagine waking up, the sun is shining, the birds are singing, your true love is by your side, and you look on the pillow – and there are a million brain cells. Those brain cells are your computer chips, and you have just lost another million. Every day you lose a million more. Whether you consciously think about it, or not, you are doomed! You cannot in any way be fundamentally optimistic if you know that your entire operating system is falling apart. This is why, as people get older, they get very frightened of the 'young stallions'. Why? Because they have more brain cells, they have more powerful bio-computers. And if you are trying to compete with them, you are obviously going to lose, unless you can manage to hold on to what you have got – and hold – and hold – until you've only got 10 brain cells left, and then you let go.

Begin to think about the attitude that is generated globally by such a belief. It is devastatingly serious. **It is like a case of intellectual Alzheimer's Disease,** which actually gets in and eats away at the intelligence. It destroys and dominates. Imagine if a World Memory Champion like Dominic O'Brien, or the world chess champion, Gary Kasparov, or a top conductor like Sir Georg Solti, were to live by this information. They are trying to hang on to their titles and their creative drive, and yet every day they may be losing a million brain cells. What would this mean to them, if it were actually true?

The evidence for this misplaced belief also comes from our social structure. What do we do with old people? We retire them! Look at the unbelievable irony. Take Jean Buzan, Tony Buzan's mother. Here she is, getting a degree in gerontology at the age of 57, lecturing at university for eight years and then being told that, because she is over 65, she is too old to talk about it! Utter lunacy. We retire people at 65, because they are 'mentally incompetent', yet at the same time we specifically leave politicians over 65 in power. It's worth investigating the logic behind these decisions.

We have retirement homes, where carers are taught how to deal with old people. We regiment them, tell them they are not sexual any longer, give them inane things like basket-weaving to do, and pat them on the head. We don't allow them to do things for themselves, because they are too old, and so they might not be able to do it. 'Don't worry – we'll do it for you. Don't get up – we'll get it for you.' We are literally killing them. A pretty depressing and horrible picture.

Let's take it apart and look at the evidence. The first thing to look at is measured decline.

If you look at the straight line (marked A), you will see that mental decline actually amounts to only 5–15 per cent over an entire lifetime. So although

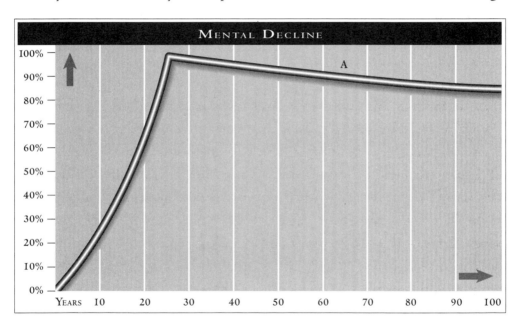

it is steady, it is not steep. It is also, actually, not new to old age. Any of you who have woken up the morning after a fantastic party will have experienced your intellectual capacities working at a level of only about 2 per cent – and that's at any age. So this is not a new experience. What is interesting about it is just how staggeringly resilient the brain is. Look how we abuse it over a lifetime, and yet it only declines by 5–15 per cent. That's extraordinary.

RENEGADES FROM THE NORM

The second, and more interesting, thing to examine is the study material on the supposed deterioration of the brain. One of the great statistical ignorances is that **the average statistic represents the average person. This just isn't true.** The average statistic is made up of those who are above average and those who are below. So, in fact, the real picture resembles a cascade, with some people whose brains show a phenomenally steep decline and others whose brains actually improve, as well as all the different experiences in between.

Those who are above average are described as statistical anomalies, and they 'mess up' the chart. These people are called 'renegades from the norm'. If you try to find common characteristics among these positive 'renegades' you do, indeed, find that they have almost identical personality profiles in the following areas. They are all interested in learning. In life, they are all positive, optimistic and in balance. They are all active, physically, mentally, emotionally, sensually and sexually. The majority of them have a highly developed sense of humour. They all tend to teach, and they also consider themselves wealthy. And there is a growing number of them.

The graph showing physical decline (opposite) looks similar to the graph of mental decline, except that it is more marked. Interestingly, here too the same misconceptions are beginning to be exposed. In terms of strength, the latest information supports the view that, if the body is trained in strength, its physical peak is reached at around the age of 50. If we look at stamina, for example, we see that long-distance marathon swimmers are usually in the 30–50

BRAIN FLASH

MARATHON WOMEN

'The oldest female athlete to complete the full distance in a marathon was 82-year-old New Zealander, Thelma Pitt-Turner, in 1987.

89-year-old Aileen Riggin Soule ought to be a household name. She is America's oldest living Olympic gold medallist, taking a gold medal in springboard diving at the Antwerp Olympics of 1920. Four years later, she was back at the Olympics in Paris, where she won a silver in springboard diving and a bronze in the 100-metre backstroke. Soule has recently set six world records in swimming for her 85–89 age group. In 1996, when she joins the over-90 group, she has announced that she plans to set some more.'

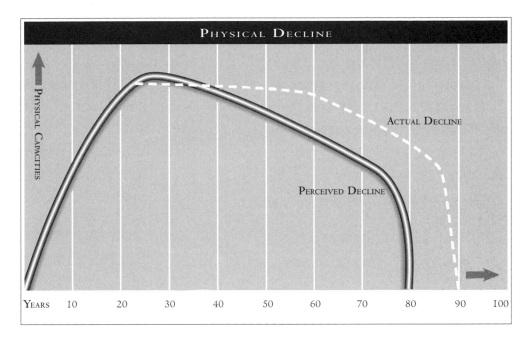

age range. So the physical graph is changing. We don't know yet exactly when physical strength begins to decline, but the rate of decline is a lot less steep than was previously thought. There are now competitions called the Veterans' Olympics, in which 80-year-olds do Olympic dives off the diving boards and run marathons, *and* do well in them.

AN EVOLUTIONARY HICCUP

Evidence now indicates that — physically, cardiovascularly, muscularly and flexibly — not much changes in the body as it ages — **as long as it is kept healthy.** So, on the physical side, we begin to see that it was assumed perceptions that had crafted the reality. With the brain, this is even more true. And what the existence of the 'renegades from the norm' suggests is that perhaps everyone can follow their example. Maybe the degeneration was just an evolutionary stage, a hiccup in time, when the brain was nurtured in such a way as to help it decline. So the experiments, in fact, prove the opposite to what everyone interprets them to prove. They do not show that the brain gets worse with

---

BRAIN FLASH

YOUR BRAIN — A POWERFUL COMPUTER

'Recent research suggests that stimulating the mind with mental exercise may cause brain cells, called neurons, to branch wildly. The branching causes millions of additional connections, or synapses, between brain cells. "Think of it," says Arnold Scheibel, Director of UCLA's [University of California at Los Angeles'] Brain Research Institute, "as a computer with a bigger memory board. You can do more things more quickly!"

The capacity of the brain to change offers new hope for preventing and treating brain diseases. It helps explain why some people can:

☆ Delay the onset of Alzheimer's Disease symptoms for years. Studies now show that the more educated a person is, the less likely he or she is to show symptoms of the disease. The reason: intellectual activity develops surplus brain tissue that compensates for tissue damaged by the disease.

☆ Make a better recovery from strokes. Research indicates that even when areas of the brain are permanently damaged by a stroke, new message routes can be created to get around the road block or to resume the function of that area.

David Snowdon of the Sanders-Brown Centre on Ageing at the University of Kentucky has found that those who earn college degrees, who teach, who constantly challenge their minds, live longer than the less educated.

New thinking in brain science suggests that whether someone hits the wall at age 65 or at age 102 may be partly up to the individual.'

---

age. They show that the human brain regularly continues to improve throughout life – under certain circumstances.

EXAGGERATED RUMOURS

Let's move on to the widespread reports about declining memory. They turn out to be an introspection based on a false piece of knowledge. There is a global society called the 'my memory is getting worse as I am getting older' club, and you hear people congratulating each other, and empathizing with each other, about how bad their memories are. And that's at 30 years old!

Now if you actually want to check your memory and take a closer look at the 'great memory' genius you used to be, go to any school at the end of the day and look at what is left behind by its young giants of learning and memory: pens, pencils, shoes, coats, etc. The only difference between a 6-year-old and a 60-year-old is that, when the 6-year-old gets home and realizes he's left his sweets, homework or whatever at school, he doesn't say to himself: 'Oh my God – I'm six years old and my memory is going', whereas the adult does. So the adult builds up a belief in the perfect memory that he or she used to have, and at the same time nurtures a belief about the failure of his or her current memory. The two build and feed on each other. **And that belief can bring down a mind. That belief could bring down a race, a planet, and could even extinguish intelligence.**

So the reports can largely be eliminated as evidence, as they are manifestly delusions. They tie in with the experiments, the experiments tie in with the reports – and so on and on they go, hand in hand, in an ever-widening circle of despair.

The social evidence can be eliminated as well. Who says that we have to put 65-year-olds into retirement? If you take the scientific approach to evolution and assume that the human race is 3 million years old, then the modern brain, with which we are all equipped, is only about 50,000 years old, which means that we have only a few generations' worth of experiments available to us. Not enough to condemn every 65-year-old and over to a life of misery.

Now, write down 10 words that you think are most commonly connected with age...

Generally we have the societal attitude that age is somehow bad, and the words that most people associate with age tend to be negative, patronizing or sickeningly euphemistic. Some of the more common ones are listed below:

☆ Sad

☆ Lonely

☆ Sick

☆ Old

☆ Poor

☆ Alone

☆ Dirty

☆ Crippled

☆ Slow

☆ Weak

☆ Pensioner

☆ Old-age pensioner

☆ Senior citizen

We want to put this into the context of a child. If a child grows up thinking these things about old age, what is he or she likely to do? Back away from it? Not think about it? What does such a belief do to the child? Just think about it for a minute.

The child won't want to see or think about old age, therefore it won't prepare for it. It will start to see all sorts of inadequacies in itself, because it is 'getting older'. That means that there will be no pro-activity towards age, because it will remind them of the horror that's approaching. Now, consider that as a global intellectual thought.

It is also a very recent state of mind, because it was not so long ago that such beliefs were *not* the norm. Write down the words that other societies gave to those people in their populations who were older, the oldest and wisest in their tribes.

Some of the words that we have collected in our research include:

☆ Sages	☆ Venerable	☆ *Troisième âge*
☆ Elders	☆ Veterans	☆ Oral historians
☆ *Paterfamilias*	☆ All-seeing	☆ Oracles
☆ Patriarchs	☆ The revered	☆ *O sensei*
☆ Matriarchs	☆ Gurus	☆ *Les vieux*

Some of these terms of respect – and belief in them – still exist today among certain societies.

Lack of Proof

This leads us to the last 'proof' – that of the brain cells dropping off. If they are the computer chips of the brain, to continue the metaphor, then that's a pretty damning piece of evidence. We are pleased to report, however, that a few years ago the *New Scientist* investigation team and the American researcher Dr Marion Diamond both asked: **'Who said that?'** The evidence was supposed to be contained in a medical text book. So they checked the references – and

---

BRAIN FLASH

AGED BRAIN AS ACTIVE AS THE YOUNG BRAIN

'A recent study of brain chemistry at the National Institute of Ageing, using a brain scan to study men whose ages ranged from 21 to 83, found that "the healthy aged brain is as active and efficient as the healthy young brain", based on the direct assessment of metabolic activity in various parts of the brain.

"What can happen," Dr Avorn said, "is that an older person who is admitted to a hospital for something like a broken hip or heart attack can become confused as a side-effect of drugs or simply from the strangeness of the hospital routine. The condition is reversible, but the family, or even the physician, doesn't recognize that fact. They assume this is the beginning of senile dementia, and pack the person off to a nursing home.

"No one knows what exact proportion of people in nursing homes needn't be there," he said, "but we have ample clinical evidence that the numbers are large."'

---

the references in those references — and it turned out, fundamentally, to be a giant circle. Everybody was quoting everybody else — and there was no basic evidence. There were suggestions, implications and hints, but there was no proof.

What researchers are now finding out is that not only does the brain *not* lose brain cells with age, but that, when it thinks appropriately, each brain cell tends to grow *more* connection points. In other words, under a certain type of positive stress the brain will generate a more sophisticated bio-computer, with more connection points and more potential, and also a greater ability to link bits of its knowledge together.

So we are at a stage when we can actively disprove all the major items of hitherto accepted 'evidence' for the brain's automatic degeneration with age.

What we are actually doing, when we talk about the human race, *Homo sapiens*, is investing hundreds of billions of pounds and dollars in the development of an intellectual system (i.e., a human being). *But*, when it reaches its peak, at 65, we say, 'Cut the system off.' This is so irrational as to be humorous. It also means that we are cutting off our collective memory, the history of our race. We are actually saying: 'Your 65 or 85 years are completely irrelevant,

---

BRAIN FLASH

The value of experience

'Many organizations are going wrong because they have lost their collective "memory" — because somewhere in the business changes that have taken place in the last 10 years, **the idea of experience has become devalued.**

Experience is now viewed negatively, because it is said to hold back the speed of change within the organization.

Lack of experienced staff helps to explain the poor performance of one UK high-street bank. According to one academic, "By sacking long-serving managers every time they [the bank] made a business mistake, **they wiped out the organizational memory and increased the chances of making further mistakes."'**

---

they don't exist or have any meaning'. Now companies are starting to do this by offering early retirement. The ironic part is that when a company does this, it has no collective memory of how it handled a particular crisis or situation, and so it has lost its intellectual capital. Therefore, when that situation occurs again it has to hire back the early retirement-takers as consultants! **The focus of this book is to say: 'Now is the time to change all that.'**

As the brain gets older it must, of necessity, get better and better, until the moment before it dies — as long as it is used well and with the right operating guide. Now we will show you how to achieve that.

THE BRAIN CELL

The brain cell, the neurone, numbers a billion in each human brain. In mathematical terms that is 10 to the power of 12, or 1 with 12 noughts after it. To grasp the magnitude of that number we want you to imagine building-blocks. Every time you add a nought, you multiply the amount by 10. So, start with 10, as a pile of imaginary bricks in front of you. Add a nought — that multiplies the pile by 10, and now you have a pile of building-bricks numbering 100 in front of you. Add another nought, and you multiply the bricks by 10 again. Now you have a pile of 1,000 bricks. One more nought and 1,000 becomes 10,000. One more nought and it becomes 100,000, and you just keep adding noughts until you get to twelve. That's the number of cells that exist in the average human brain.

FIAT LUX – LET THERE BE LIGHT

The power of the brain cell is extraordinary. The more we have investigated it, the more we have realized that the power is greater than we thought. Let's just look at what one brain cell can do. One brain cell, genetically, holds the code for the perfect duplication of yourself in its memory. Think of the amount of information that it contains in order to do this. It's like a gigantic library, and that is only one tiny part of what it can do. It is considerably more powerful than any computer. One interesting fact: in your head there exists the potential for more human beings than there are on the planet. So you contain a planet's worth of potential humans in your own head!

Tiny living beings, like bees, have identical brain cells to us. The difference is that they have only a few thousand, yet look what they can do. They can smell, they can see, they can navigate, they can remember and communicate with each other. Research shows that insects like the bee have one brain cell that becomes like the godfather of the brain. It seems that one cell is the boss. This brain cell is no different from any of the others, it just shows the potential that lies within each cell. That's the power of the brain cell, and we have a billion of them.

Each cell acts like a system on its own. It extends and seeks others to connect to. And it is this seeking for connections that is important. If you could see the brain, you would actually see the biggest cuddle in the world. Each brain cell wraps its tentacles round all the others, to create a package of interconnectivity. Along each tentacle there are little mushrooms (a good simile would be an octopus sucker) and there are tens of thousands of these found on each tentacle, and there are tens of thousands of tentacles, all connecting in millions of different ways. Inside each mushroom, on each tentacle, there are thousands of chemical formulae. Whenever you think, whatever you think, an electromagnetic, biochemical reaction results from this. An impulse goes down one branch of one brain cell, for reasons we don't yet know and in ways we don't yet understand. Each one of these brain cells is independent – each one makes its own decisions about where the message goes. Although it's totally interdependent on the other cells, it is also completely independent at the same time. When a message comes down the tentacle and reaches the mushroom, a chemical cocktail is fired across the gap to the next mushroom on the next cell. This gap is called the synaptic gap.

So there is a pathway, which is known as a 'trace of memory', a memory trace. It is an incredible, yet real, pattern of thought. It is a map of intellectual territory, it is a habit, and it is a probability. It is all these things at the same time, and it is real.

When it first starts to grow, in a baby, the brain cell has a fundamental structure and growth. If a baby is not stimulated, it will simply tread intellectual water. The brain cells do not connect and grow of their own accord. Stimulation is the key food for growth of the organ and its complexity. It isn't the size of the cell that's important, but rather its interconnectivity and its sophistication.

THE LIMITS OF LEARNING

The question, then, about the limits of human learning – the ability of the human to learn over time and through age – can be reduced, on one level, to a mathematical equation. How many brain cells are available? How many thoughts can the brain take in? Its limited capacity is often given as a reason for people to stop learning: 'I am not going to learn any more, as my brain is almost full up and I need to save the space.' This kind of excuse for inaction is ludicrous. We have written *The Age Heresy* to counter this notion.

So how many thought traces can we make? In the 1950s the number of thought traces was calculated to be 10 to the power of 100. After a period of time this number was revised to 10 to the power of 800. That number turned out to be incorrect yet again, and the new number calculated by Professor P. Anokhin for the potential patterns of thought was *minimally* I followed by 6.5 million miles (10.5 million km) of typewritten noughts. **So our capacity is functionally limitless.** And the potential for someone like Dominic O'Brien to become World Memory Champion at the age of 95, having memorized the entire history of the world, actually exists, mathematically.

META-POSITIVE THINKING: THE POWER TO CHANGE YOURSELF FOR THE BETTER

What is remarkable about the thought process is that it drives itself. So let's look at a brain thought *in situ*. Let's take a brain cell, and let's take a habit that links this brain cell to many others. This is a BBH, a Big Bad Habit, one that is counterproductive to your survival. It's one you are aware of and have decided to change. Let's imagine this habit is eating two boxes of chocolates per day, that you weigh 400 lb (181 kg) and have been doing this for 20 years.

It could equally be a BBH that is going to take 12 years off your life, such as smoking 40 cigarettes a day; or 8 years off, such as an Olympic gold-medal-winning level of alcohol intake; and so on… but let's stay with the chocolate analogy for the moment.

What's the first thing that comes into your mind when you say: 'I am *not* going to eat *chocolates*'? Notice the *first* thing that occurs to you when you even read that phrase — was it not the chocolates themselves? Did you see the packaging of your favourite ones?

CHANGING YOURSELF FOR THE BETTER — HOW TO USE META-POSITIVE THINKING TO DESIGN YOUR OWN AGEING STRATEGY

So, a thought is whizzing through the circuits of your brain. It has run through many times before, for it is a habit, something you don't even think about — it is subconscious and **now you are trying to change it, consciously.** The good news is that even thinking 'I am going to change' actually does change the brain on a physiological level, causing different traces to activate through your brain cells. But — and it's a big but — a habit is something you have been doing for years, and along comes a birthday and someone gives you — chocolates. What are you thinking now, as you look at the box? Possibly 'I'll just have one!'

This is a BBH, a Big Bad Habit; it took years to install it in your mental software, so is it logical to think that you can change it all at once? But, bit by bit, every time you re-commit to your goal you can install new thought patterns and make new positive thoughts the GNH (Good New Habit).

META-POSITIVE THINKING: THE KEY STEPS

How do you do this? The best way is by deciding what to focus on and then by re-committing to it regularly. In the chocolate example, where was your focus? It was on the chocolates, wasn't it? So a more appropriate way of getting a handle on the subject would be to think about what you might gain by not eating chocolates. Your ultimate goal in conquering your Big Bad Habit and establishing a Good New Habit is to become fitter and healthier. How could we actually describe this goal? To be really effective, an affirmation has to fulfil the following criteria:

✩ It must be personal – I…
✩ It must be stated in the present – I am…
✩ It must cover the process of what you are doing. This is important, because if you say to yourself, 'I am healthy', and you aren't, you are actually lying to yourself, so – I am becoming…
✩ It must contain the goal within it – I am becoming healthy.

Re-committing to this goal regularly will help your brain re-wire its BBH into a GNH. The illustration opposite shows graphically the jaws of a Big Bad Habit

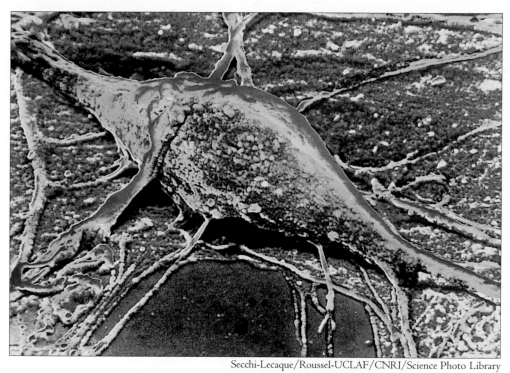

Secchi-Lecaque/Roussel-UCLAF/CNRI/Science Photo Library

ABOVE: Each brain cell reaches out to other cells, firing a 'chemical cocktail' across the synaptic gap between cells, so creating a real trace of memory.

RIGHT: The brain cells of inactive rats (below) have few hairlike dendrites surrounding them, whereas those of active rats (above) show far more dendritic growth, allowing many more connections with other brain cells.

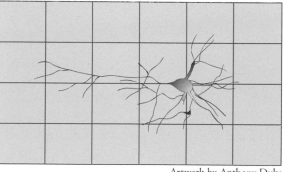

Artwork by Anthony Duke

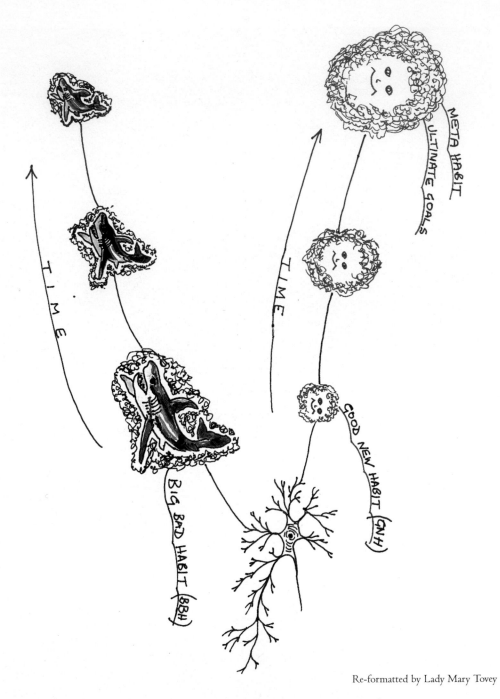

Re-formatted by Lady Mary Tovey

ABOVE: A graphic representation of the 'Jaws of a Big Bad Habit', and how a Good New Habit builds up as you nurture its power.

Re-formatted by Lady Mary Tovey

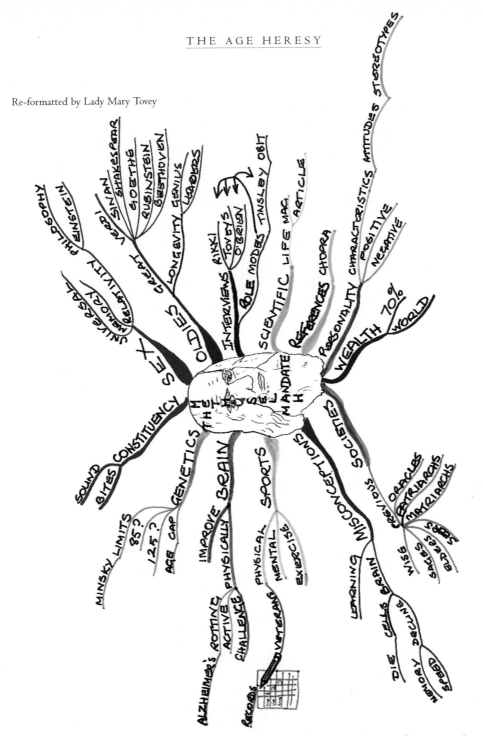

ABOVE: The message of 'The Methuselah Mandate', as shown in this Mind Map, is that your brain can, as you age, become increasingly sophisticated, if you stimulate it and transform harmful habits.

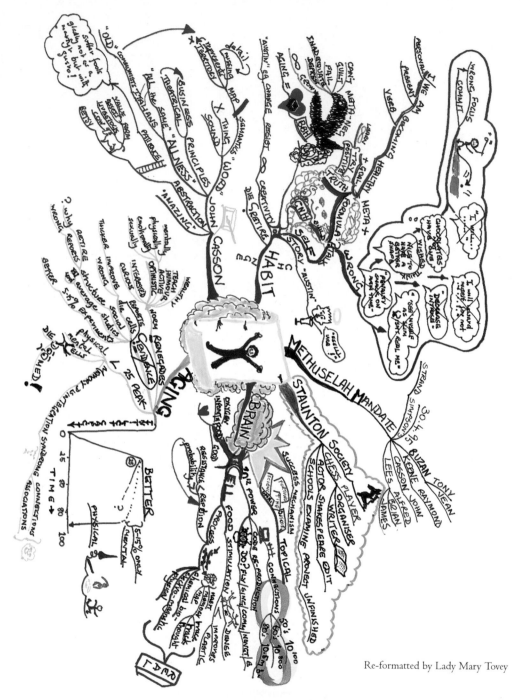

ABOVE: *This Mind Map of Tony Buzan's Methuselah lecture spells out the benefits of TEFCAS and of turning a Big Bad Habit into a Good New Habit.*

Re-formatted by Lady Mary Tovey

and how your Good New Habits build up as you nurture their power. This is called meta-positive thinking or – thinking for a change for the better.

A graphic representation of the 'Jaws of a Big Bad Habit'.

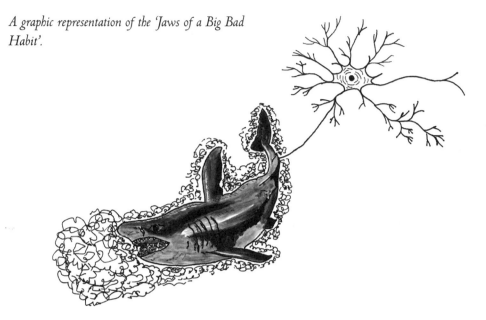

THE META-POSITIVE APPROACH TO AGEING

How is this applicable to ageing? The thoughts you have about ageing could be part of the BBH or the GNH. Which one would you like it to be? **And, most importantly, in the context of designing strategies for successful ageing, consider this.** If you are trying to:

☆ start doing aerobic exercise (e.g. rowing, swimming, running, cycling), *where previously you were doing none...*
☆ change or improve an *unhealthy* diet in order to improve your fitness and stamina...
☆ *give up* smoking... or *excessive* drinking...
☆ develop your powers of memory, or take up a *challenging new mental exercise,* or develop a new mental skill, such as mind sports, chess, 'Go' or Mind Mapping...
☆ learn swimming or juggling or a martial art...

then our message on the transformation of a BIG BAD HABIT into a GOOD NEW HABIT is of central significance to you!

THE NEXT META-POSITIVE STEP: TEFCAS

TEFCAS is a mnemonic devised by Tony Buzan to reflect how the brain learns and to help you remember this easily. To understand how TEFCAS works, let's take a concrete example. We teach 'Go', chess, mind sports and juggling at our seminars as a metaphor for learning. Juggling often strikes particular terror into the audience! When first confronted by the balls, many a stout-hearted individual has been seen to back away – even physically. The first throw may be successful or not – but how do you judge if it was successful if you have nothing to compare it with? You might look around and see how others are doing. If you were having limited success you might give up quickly.

Your individual approach to learning, and how you process events, is the key to successful ageing.

So how *do* you learn? Over the past ten years we have been collecting people's views from around the world and they are generally the same. Illustrated below is the graphic representation of those views. It suggests that everyone learns and acquires new or changed habits in a smooth curve.

How completely wrong this illusion is! Yet it is extremely powerful and pervasive, in all cultures and all languages.

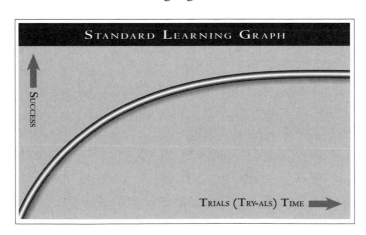

The brain has a very specific procedure for learning and the integration of new skills, and we will use the TEFCAS mnemonic to spell it out:

T is for Trial. You try something new: juggling, eating more healthily, cutting back on drinking, eliminating smoking, starting aerobic exercise, etc. Keeping interested and challenging your brain is part of trying something.

E is for Event. Something happens. You catch the ball, or you don't. These are just events, not success or failure on their own. Divorcing the emotion from an event means that you can continue, when others have 'failed'. It also means that you can apply clear criteria as to what has happened, be it a 'good' event, or a 'bad' one. You can learn from the data, without the labels of judgement.

F is for Feedback. How did you do? Getting appropriate feedback means that you will be able to assess accurately and plan your next stage…

C is for Check. Check it out against someone else – a professional, or even your teacher, or against your own goals…

A is for Adjust. It was once said that the definition of madness was to carry on doing something, while expecting a different result. So if what you are doing doesn't work, opt for a changed approach – a different teacher, different type of equipment.

S is for SUCCESS. Time for celebration, giving the brain something to look forward to when it succeeds, which it will when it follows the correct formulae.

'Es irrt der Mensch, so lang er strebt.'
'Whilst striving to achieve, mistakes are inevitable.'

JOHANN WOLFGANG VON GOETHE

The illustration overleaf shows how the brain learns, with its plateaux, troughs and peaks. Next time you do something new, look at this chart to establish where you are in your learning. Do not be discouraged if you sometimes seem to be failing. This is normal and natural in the learning or changing process.

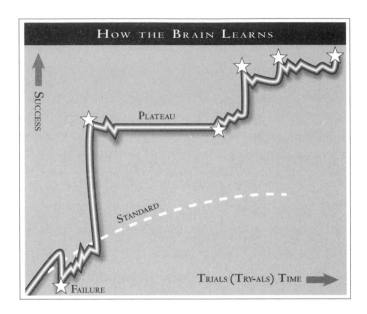

In your own process for successful ageing one possible meta-positive process — or change for the better — based on smoking (from infinite Big Bad possibilities, such as excessive eating or drinking, or taking no exercise), might look like this:

A TYPICAL META-POSITIVE PROGRESSION USING TEFCAS

1. TRIAL	Constantly feeling below par.
2. EVENT	Smoking 40 cigarettes per day.
3. FEEDBACK	Told by experts that this habit will reduce your life-expectancy by 12 years.
4. CHECK	Go for second opinion and advice.
5. ADJUST	Gradually cut down on smoking. There will be peaks and troughs.
6. Success	Gradually — but steadily — become more healthy.

BRAIN FLASH

NICOTINE IMPAIRS BRAIN CELLS

Research indicates that nicotine impairs, rather than stimulates, brain cells, contrary to earlier belief, and this may explain the drug's calming effect, Linda Wong of the University of Texas/Galveston has stated. Wong claimed that nicotine appeared to suppress the rat brain cells that control basic behaviour, such as learning, memory and emotion. Her experiments and conclusions were presented at the 40th annual meeting of the American Society for Pharmacology and Experimental Therapeutics in August 1989. Her findings contradicted the traditional scientific belief that nicotine stimulates brains cells.

For years scientists believed that the drug excites some neurones, which in turn inhibit other brain functions to induce a calming effect on smokers. Wong said that her studies on rats suggested that nicotine directly reduces neurone activity in human beings. Her findings were based on a two-year study, in which nicotine was applied to tissue removed from the base of rats' brains.

Wong was originally researching the mechanisms that control a neurone receptor linked to the theta rhythm, an electrical current produced by the brain. It was only by chance that she and her colleagues noticed that **nicotine actually restrains neural activity.** *'It was startling and surprising,' she said. She found that nicotine makes it more difficult to fire signals to other neurones, because the drug causes the affected neurone to release potassium, which plays a critical inhibiting role in the transmission of nervous impulses. Another explanation for the apparent 'calming' effect of cigarettes in some smokers is that they may, each time they inhale, be suffering a 'mini-faint', due to momentary lack of oxygen to the lungs and brain.*

These findings are entirely in line with our life-expectancy calculations in Chapter Two, where we gave this clear warning: **Take off 12 years from your standard life-expectancy if you smoke more than 40 cigarettes a day.**

THE META-POSITIVE MESSAGE: IT'S NEVER TOO LATE (OR TOO EARLY) TO START

'Learn everything! Later you will see that nothing is superfluous.'

PRIOR HUGH OF ST VICTOR, FL. TWELFTH CENTURY

'Everything connects to everything else.'

LEONARDO DA VINCI

You now are armed with such phenomenal new information that it is possible for you actually to **expand your own brain!**

It is time, therefore, to begin.

BRAIN STORM: GOLDEN RULES

1. Believe in your brain and its capacity.

2. Study it at every level, from its biophysiology and neurochemistry to its huge range of mental skills. Understand both meta-positive thinking and TEFCAS.

3. Cherish it.

4. Use it. As Leonardo da Vinci said, in his own laws for developing a 'complete' brain:

☆ Study the science of art.

☆ Study the art of science.

☆ Learn how to see/develop your senses.

☆ **Practise the previous three in the context of the realization that everything connects to everything else.**

By learning how your own brain works, you will simultaneously be encouraging it to perform better. For example, when you learn and fully realize that one of your brain's prime 'skills' is imagination, combined with association, the mere fact of knowing this will automatically set your brain on a path on which it will use these two skills more.

To enhance this process it is useful, once you have learnt about the basic and extraordinarily subtle mechanics of your brain, to learn specific skills, such as Mind Mapping, memory techniques, creative thinking, speed-reading and a full range of physical skills. The more you learn about your brain and about how to use it well, the more you will create a positive spiral in all areas of your development. **For example, the knowledge that there is no brain cell loss with age in normal, active and healthy brains can be extra-**

ordinarily motivating and encouraging. We now move on to the most commonly asked question among reader groups and audiences in the 40–50-plus age range:

Q: How can I improve my collapsing and failing memory?

For instance, you may often have been given a telephone number and forgotten it within two minutes, or have been introduced to 10 people and forgotten their names within seconds of being introduced to the tenth. **Older people often see this as evidence of their declining mental powers. However, the syndrome is just as common in the young as in the old.**

A: Long-term memory is that process which is so 'automatic' that many people don't even realize that it is memory. For example, every word of every language you speak daily is a function of your long-term memory. It is also an example of the incredible ongoing power and accuracy of these mental skills.

One often hears people complaining vociferously about their declining mental powers as they age and, in particular, bemoaning their vanishing powers of memory. Yet they do this with a coherence, eloquence and masterful recall of language that utterly refutes the point they are trying to make!

Your name, the vast ranges of your 'standard' knowledge, and your memory of environments and routes are also part of your long-term memory. Both short- and long-term memory can be improved by practising your powers of concentration, association, imagination and, as da Vinci suggested, by developing each of your senses. When developed in such a way, each helps the other, and all help you.

WHAT SHOULD I DO NOW?

1. If you don't already exercise, now is the time to start, now that you know how your brain accepts a Good New Habit.

2. In forthcoming chapters we give tips on diet. Think about yours — is it unhealthy? Lots of junk food and sugary snacks? If so, now that you know how to ditch the Big Bad Habit this is the time for change!

3. Similarly, use TEFCAS and your new knowledge of the BBH and GNH to commit to becoming healthier in every way. Your mental powers will improve and you will live longer to enjoy exercising them.

4. If you wish to develop a particular new mental skill, such as your powers of memory, you now know how to convince your brain to start the learning process. The meta-positive thinking we have described is the way forward.

5. Having established the possibility of developing the brain through stimulation, it is essential, next, to search for a moral or ethical theory that effectively supports the physiological thesis. The next chapter does just this.

BRAIN FLASH

BUILDING A BETTER BRAIN

Neuroscientists explore the benefits of brain callisthenics. How you can think faster, improve your memory and defend against Alzheimer's Disease.

"Evidence is accumulating that the brain works a lot like a muscle — the harder you use it, the more it grows. Although scientists had long believed the brain's circuitry was hard-wired by adolescence and inflexible in adulthood, it's newly discovered ability to change and adapt is apparently with us well into old age. Best of all, this research has opened up an exciting world of possibilities for treating strokes and head injuries — and warding off Alzheimer's Disease."'

CHAPTER FIVE

THE GOETHE GAUNTLET

—

'WER IMMER STREBEND SICH BEMÜHT, DEN KÖNNEN WIR ERLÖSEN.'
'STRIVING TO ACHIEVE IS THE PATH TO SALVATION.'

'AM ANFANG WAR DAS WORT? AM ANFANG WAR DIE TAT!'
'IN THE BEGINNING WAS THE WORD? IN THE BEGINNING WAS THE DEED!'

JOHANN WOLFGANG VON GOETHE, *FAUST*

INTRODUCTION

We have now discovered that the physiological stimulation of the brain produces dramatic and advantageous changes. The next logical step is to search for an artistic, literary, political and philosophical basis for the physiological fact – a 'Philosophy of Stimulation'.

The writings of Goethe, one of the greatest geniuses of all time, provide the philosophical justification for a strategy of self-improvement through self-challenge. We quote and reinterpret key lines from Goethe's masterwork *Faust* to do this. The element of self-challenge is crucial, since this is the way to develop the new synaptic connections that physically improve your brain.

THE CHALLENGE THAT IS THE KEY TO THIS BOOK

Johann Wolfgang von Goethe (1749–1832) was, and is, for German culture an amalgam of Shakespeare, Milton, Byron, Dante, Racine, Corneille and Moliere, all rolled into one. Renowned, on account of his gigantic active vocabulary of 50,000 words, as the man with the highest IQ in the history of the planet, Goethe was, in his day, lawyer, poet, dramatist, novelist, statesman, historian, anatomist, botanist, optician and philosopher. Pursuing each separate career simultaneously, but with equal commitment and energy, he lived to the healthy age of 83, and died still striving for the maximum, with the significant words *'Mehr Licht'* – 'More Light' – on his lips.

Goethe's supreme masterwork was his tragedy *Faust*, written in two parts. This gigantic epic poem, the greatest dramatic work in German literature, tells the story of Faust, the scientist/philosopher who, in order to pierce the only mysteries still unfathomed by his research, sells his soul to the Devil (Mephistopheles) to win total knowledge and absolute power. The Faust tragedy is a theme that has powerfully attracted other world-class writers, such as Christopher Marlowe and Thomas Mann, representing, as it does, one of the most potent myths of Western civilization. But Goethe put a very different slant on it, one that explains his own enormous creative output over such a long life, and one that contains a massively important message for us.

Goethe first set out his extensive plan for *Faust* Part I in 1797, at the age of 48. He spent the remainder of his life working on *Faust*, and it was the final major piece of writing he completed, at the age of 82, in 1831, just nine months before his death.

In *Buzan's Book of Genius* we presented for the first time the theory of Goethendipity, a vital secret known to all possessors of genius. Here we re-state this formula in Goethe's own words. Its effectiveness will be immediately apparent to all readers who are determined to improve their own performance, at any age, and in any walk of life.

Over to Goethe:

IN THE BEGINNING WAS THE DEED!

'Until one is committed, there is hesitancy, the chance to draw back, always ineffectiveness. Concerning all acts of initiative (and creation), there is one elementary truth, the ignorance of which kills countless ideas and splendid plans: that the moment one definitely commits oneself, then providence moves too.

'All sorts of things occur to help one, that would never otherwise have occurred. A whole stream of events issues from the decision, raising in one's favour all manner of unforeseen incidents and meetings and material assistance, which no man could have dreamed would have come his way.

'Whatever you can do, or dream you can, begin it. Boldness has genius, power and magic in it. Begin it now.'

Now, for the first time, we reveal the hidden meaning behind the central passage in *Faust*. **We call this 'The Goethe Gauntlet' and it embodies the one central truth for all those of you who wish to improve the power and efficiency of your brains as you age.**

Make no mistake, this is not a chimera designed to produce an artificial sense of well-being in a gullible audience. It is a well-attested medical fact, confirmed by the well-known Harley Street specialist, Dr Andrew Strigner, among others. The synaptic connections in your brain grow and actually physically improve their powers of association, if you present constant fresh challenges to your thinking apparatus.

Constantly seek out fresh stimuli and exciting challenges, and your life will become richer, more interesting, more fun and – ultimately – more full of meaning.

HERE IS HOW YOU CAN DO IT

Once again, over to Goethe. We have reached that scene in *Faust* where the Devil offers Faust every pleasure a human being could possibly desire. Here is Faust's sensational and significant reaction:

FAUST: 'Should I ever lay myself on a bed of ease, then let life be over for me! If you can ever delude me that I have no ambitions left, if you can entice me with a life of pure pleasure, that will be my last day on earth! This is my Challenge!'

DEVIL: 'Agreed!'

FAUST: 'Confirmed, not once, but twice! Should I ever say of a particular moment – tarry, you are so precious, at that instant, clap me in your

devil's chains, for I will have lost my great game. The death knell may toll for me then and you will be free of your service. The clock will stop, the hour hand fall and, for me, time will be over!'
(translation from Goethe's *Faust* especially for this book by Ray Keene)

This message colours and informs every single piece of advice we offer in this book. The message is, in fact, designed specifically for those of you who want to improve your brains as you age and not see your mental faculties disintegrate.

Goethe's message, as expressed in those few lines, is one of tireless endeavour, of constant striving. But it must be purposeful and positive effort, pursuing its course in the full consciousness of our place within the grand context of the universe. In this sense, *Faust* is a poem of supreme optimism – it was Goethe's testament to his nation and to the world. As critics have noted, by reason of its sublimely universal content, its breadth of emotional and intellectual appeal, and its wealth and variety of poetic form, *Faust* has earned the right to be placed alongside Virgil's *Aeneid*, Dante's *Divine Comedy* and Milton's *Paradise Lost.*

Before you embark on the rest of this book – always bearing at the forefront of your mind the Goethean message, through which to view all the forthcoming information, advice and exercises – it is worth mentioning a possible philosophical counter-argument.

THE VOLTAIREAN COUNTER-GAMBIT?

The great French writer and philosopher Voltaire (1694–1778) famously, in his book *Candide*, offered this piece of metaphorical advice for those of advancing years:

'Il faut cultiver notre jardin!'
'We must cultivate our garden.'

This, at first sight, anodyne exhortation seems far removed from Goethe's message of constant striving, but look more closely. Voltaire did not write: 'We must retire to our garden'; or 'We must fall asleep in our garden'; or 'We must smoke pot in our garden'; and especially he did not write: 'We must drink ourselves senseless in our garden.'

Voltaire deliberately, consciously and subtly used the active word 'cultivate', and in that sense he was at one with Goethe.

WHAT SHOULD I DO NOW?

1. Be mentally active. Choose an interesting and challenging goal and achieve it. What are your interests? What are you good at? What do you enjoy doing? Choose a challenge from one of your best fields.

2. Learn dancing; study a new language; play a musical instrument; take up mind sports; start painting. There are dozens of sports to choose from: sailing, mountain biking, athletics, martial arts, the choice is infinite. Even cross Antarctica or climb Mount Everest if you feel really adventurous! The important thing — no matter how great or small the challenge — is to stimulate yourself. If at the same time you can become socially involved with other people and adapt to new situations as they arise, so much the better.

BRAIN FLASH

STIMULUS V. STAGNATION

To assess the effect of a rich environment on brain growth, Mark Rosenzweig, of the University of California at Berkeley, allowed a group of baby rats to grow up in a cage full of ramps, ladders, wheel, tunnels and other stimuli. A second group was left in barren cages. After 105 days the brains were examined, showing that the brains of the rats raised in the rich environment were larger than those of the control group. There were also 15 per cent more glia cells, and the neuron bodies were 15 per cent larger, and, perhaps most importantly, there were more interconnections with other neurons. **By now, you should be well and truly familiar with the ramifications of this particular piece of good news.**

CHAPTER SIX

THE FIRST CHALLENGE

'MOST NOBLE EMPEROR, IF EVER A MAN COULD ESCAPE DEATH BY LEARNING, THEN YOU
WOULD BE THE ONE!'

MICHAEL SCOTT, SCHOLAR AND ASTROLOGER TO THE HOLY ROMAN EMPEROR, FREDERICK II

INTRODUCTION

We have seen from 'The Methuselah Mandate' that the brain can change physiologically, and from 'The Goethe Gauntlet' that there is a philosophical justification for pursuing this stratagem. In this chapter we offer a stimulating menu of challenges, designed to help you take the first steps on the path towards expanding your mental powers, developing the physiological complexity and sophistication of your brain, and accepting The Goethe Gauntlet.

The 10 criteria for the 'Brain of the Year' Award are set out here as personal challenges and goals representing your first step on this path. Profiles of some winners of the award are given as inspirational examples.

HIGH GOALS AND STANDARDS TO SET YOURSELF

Set yourself the ultimate challenge, the goal of being short-listed for, or indeed winning, the Brain Trust Charity's prestigious 'Brain of the Year' Award.

The Brain Trust is a charitable organization, dedicated to research and the dissemination of knowledge about cognition, learning and the brain.

The award, which has, in previous years, been given to Gary Kasparov, the world chess champion, and Dr Marion Tinsley, who defeated the Silicon Graphics Chinook computer, is presented annually to the individual who best meets the following criteria:

THE CANDIDATES:

1. Must be pre-eminent in their chosen field of endeavour.

2. Must have contributed major new creative developments to their field of endeavour.

3. Must have made a notable effort to educate other people in their chosen discipline.

4. Must have incorporated the principle of *mens sana in corpore sano* (a healthy mind in a healthy body) in their lives.

5. Must have exhibited persistence and stamina over time.

6. Must have demonstrated a general cultural awareness.

7. Must have contributed demonstrably to their society.

8. Must have shown a concern for humanity.

9. Must strive to be active, and must be known for the enthusiasm of their message.

10. Must be a good role-model, both for those in their own field of endeavour and in general.

These 10 criteria are superbly challenging goals and standards to set yourself and by which to rate your own performance and improvement in your chosen fields of lifelong endeavour.

PREVIOUS WINNERS INCLUDE:

GENE RODDENBERRY (WINNER 1992)

Well into his fifties Gene Roddenberry, the originator and mastermind behind *Star Trek*, was an engineer, decorated war hero, pilot, social mover and shaker, and visionary. In his early writing career he was the prime creative and driving force behind the cult Western *Have Gun, Will Travel*, the first Western to feature an intellectual hero, Paladin (the name for the knight chess piece). Roddenberry, who was a leading member of the American Humanist Association, moved on from there to the creation of *Star Trek*, meeting apparently insuperable barriers to putting on a television series that was initially almost universally ridiculed. The themes that inspired *Star Trek* included racial and sexual equality, the training of the intellect and the body, and the importance of compassion and love.

In Roddenberry's own words:

'To be different is not necessarily to be ugly; to have a different idea is not necessarily to be wrong. The worst possible thing that can happen to humanity is for all of them to begin to look and talk and act and think alike. **The best measure of maturity and wisdom in a human is the recognition of the value received in hearing another say, "I disagree with you for the following reasons..."'**

DOMINIC O'BRIEN (JOINT WINNER 1994)

The first World Memory Champion has maintained his dominance of the memory world since first winning the championship in 1991, setting, in the process, new world records for the perfect memorization of a 52-deck pack of cards in 2 minutes 29 seconds. In 1994 he established yet another new world record of 44.78 seconds. **He has become one of the new international brain stars, starting at an age (late thirties) when Academia maintains that creativity has already been on the wane for some time.**

A relatively unsuccessful student in school, O'Brien has dedicated his life to exploring and developing his own memory, and to helping other people learn to do the same.

DR MARION TINSLEY (WINNER 1995)

Dr Marion Tinsley, born on 3 February 1927, was for over 40 years the dominant champion of the world in the game of draughts. His greatest achievement was beating the Chinook draughts computer in London in 1992. He died on 3 April 1995.

During Tinsley's span as the dominant draughts practitioner he contested thousands of top-level tournament games and many one-on-one matches at local, national and world championships. Throughout, Tinsley lost the unbelievably small total of only nine games. According to co-author chess Grand Master Ray Keene, 'Apart from Tinsley being the supreme world record-holder in draughts, his accomplishments more than matched the greatest feats of all the giants of the chess world, including Alekhine, Fischer and Kasparov.' Tinsley was undoubtedly the greatest mind sports champion of all time, and may justifiably claim to have been the greatest champion of *any* sport.

As Tinsley was always delighted to point out, Asa Long, the former world champion and Tinsley's mentor, estimated that Tinsley had spent 100,000 hours studying draughts. Said Tinsley, 'That fact alone should answer a few questions about this "simple" game.'

By 1954 Tinsley was the undisputed world champion and No.1, although many draughts historians believe that his real domination started a good seven years earlier. **His domination of the game for the following 38 years was so complete that by 1992, at the age of 65, he had completely run out of opposition and decided to retire as undefeated champion. In recognition**

of his greatness, the draughts world bestowed upon him the title of World Champion Emeritus.

Tinsley's retirement was 'disturbed' by the arrival on the draughts scene of a phenomenally brilliant new player who cut a devastating swathe through the draughts world and became the world's new No.1. Intrigued by this new genius, Tinsley accepted a world-title challenge from the prodigy, and thus launched a new era in mind sports.

For this new player had a silicon brain. It was a Silicon Graphics computer, code-named Chinook, programmed by Professor Jonathan Schaeffer of Edmonton University in Canada. The computer could calculate an incredible three million moves a minute and had a data-base of 18 *billion* positions, including all of Tinsley's greatest games. Before the match, most mind sports players and observers exhibited extreme nervousness, afraid that the 'Silicon Brain' was going to devastate the human brain and somehow make the latter subservient.

Tinsley, in his typically calm and serene manner, appeared simply amused. When asked by the Press whether or not he was afraid of his prodigious opponent, Tinsley explained that he considered it to be very much like a post-graduate student: 'Very bright, very dedicated, willing to work on problems all night while I sleep — but can't really *think*.' He went on to explain that he felt supremely confident because, 'brilliant though Professor Schaeffer and his team are as programmers, I believe I have a superior programmer — his name is God.'

Playing draughts at a level never seen before, Tinsley, at the age of 66, gradually dominated the mechanical mind. He won the 39th game after having played four games a day for as much as 12 hours a day, for two solid weeks — a superhuman feat. This exhibited Tinsley's extraordinary will-power and stamina, as well as his belief that the human brain improves its abilities with age, especially when used well.

On the computer's resignation, Tinsley rose out of his seat exclaiming, 'A victory for human beings.'

Perhaps the greatest compliment paid to Dr Tinsley came from Professor

Schaeffer and the Grand Master draughts community. When analysing the games between Tinsley and the Chinook, they all came to an extraordinary conclusion: that if one had not known which was the computer and which the human, the sheer perfection of Tinsley's games would have convinced the knowing observer that the computer's games were those of the human and Tinsley's the product of a perfect intelligence.

As a result of his unprecedented mental accomplishments, Tinsley was nominated for, and won, the Brain Trust Charity's 'Brain of The Year' Award, which was announced at the Royal Albert Hall Festival of the Mind on 21 April 1995.

WHAT SHOULD I DO NOW?

You may decide to go in for the 'Brain of the Year' Award in a formal way, or not. However, by following the 10 criteria and challenges for candidates, which we have set out in this chapter, you will have created for yourself a clear programme, with lucidly stated goals and stages. This will lead to ongoing self-improvement. Try each challenge in turn or simultaneously.

In the next chapter we face one of the greatest challenges — the all-pervading belief that sexual activity dwindles to zero with advancing age.

BRAIN FLASH

GEORGIAN CLAIMS DISPELLED

'It has often been claimed that the State of Georgia in the former USSR produced a world-record number of gerontological marvels. This has now been unmasked as Soviet propaganda!

"Soviet officials made a point of discovering centenarians in order to gratify Stalin's pride in his native land and understandable terror of death. Even at the time, sceptics observed that the average life-span of Georgians was lower than in the Soviet Union as a whole. It has been noted that, since Stalin's death, the incidence of alleged centenarians in Georgia has declined from a torrent to a drip."'

CHAPTER SEVEN

SEX AND AGE

—

'GIVE ME CHASTITY AND CONTINENCY, BUT NOT YET.'
ST AUGUSTINE

INTRODUCTION

Does sexual activity decline with age – or is it better at 70? In this chapter we explore the fallacy that sexual activity has to decline. Sex is both a physical and mental activity, and we show how love acts as a vital brain 'food'. If you stay active, alert and curious about life, then there is no reason why sex-through-the-decades is doomed – in fact, it can be a source of ever-increasing pleasure!

A SEMINAL AND SEXY STORY

In a rest home for the over-eighties in Vancouver, British Columbia, the nurses and staff were having particular difficulty with a 92-year-old inmate. He was a wealthy man, occupying a private suite.

He was the apotheosis of the nightmare resident: truculent, intractable, grumpy, irritable, verbally abusive, permanently dissatisfied and, when not expressing his anger or dissatisfaction, seriously uncommunicative. His behaviour became particularly obnoxious during visiting times, when he was often the only resident without relatives or friends coming to see him.

One day, he asked one of the few nurses with whom he ever communicated if he might arrange for his young niece to visit him. Permission was naturally granted, and on the next visiting day (there were three per week) a vibrant, attractive young woman came to see him. After his niece's visit, the nonagenarian's demeanour perked up considerably, and arrangements were made for his niece to visit him thrice weekly. Her articulate, intelligent and friendly behaviour animated the staff and other patients as well, and her thrice-weekly visits over a period of six months transformed the home.

In particular, the man's behaviour became the opposite of what it had been before. Obviously warmed by the affection of a committed family member and stimulated by her lively personality, he became unusually sociable, chatting and bantering with staff and other patients, far more physically and mentally active, and in general a delight to be with.

This happy idyll came to a tragic end when someone inadvertently discovered the 'horrible truth': that the gentleman's 'niece' was in fact a high-class courtesan, and that rather than simply enjoying stimulating conversations three times a week, the 92-year-old sexual athlete had been having passionate love-making sessions instead!

The reactions to these findings were immediate and dramatic. The man was privately and publicly berated for being a 'dirty old man', his 'niece' was banned for ever from the home, and he was placed in virtual solitary confinement by everyone in, and connected with, the home.

Predictably, his behaviour immediately reverted to its former truculence, and the rest of his short life (arguably far shorter than it should have been) was spent in defiance and misery.

SEXUAL PERCEPTION: SEXUAL REALITY

The above story raises a number of moral issues. It also raises a number of intriguing and probing questions:

1. Why is our attitude to sex and ageing one in which sexual interest and activity become increasingly seen as 'dirty' as we get older?

2. Is it natural for men and women to experience strong sexual urges well into their later years?

3. What are the actual patterns of sexual behaviour in the human species as it advances through the years?

DECADE	RANKING FOR SEXUAL ACTIVITY
0–10	
10–20	
20–30	
30–40	
40–50	
50–60	
60–70	
70–80	
80–90	
90–100	

Tony Buzan has conducted surveys over the last 10 years into public assumptions about sexual activity. For your own enlightenment, complete the following quiz:

In the table on the left, rank, in numerical order, from 1 to 10, the decade during which you think *most* sexual activity occurs, the one in which second most activity occurs, third most activity occurs, and so on, until you rank a decade 10, indicating that the least sexual activity occurs then.

You might now wish to compare your own thoughts with Tony Buzan's global surveys. These were carried out in over 50 countries throughout Europe, the Middle East, Australasia and the Americas. The results (below) were surprisingly consistent across language and culture.

These are the general assumptions, although it was often assumed that from 60 – and even 50 onwards – there was no sexual activity or drive at all. What are the facts?

SEXUAL FACTS/TRENDS

Even with Freud's purported 'liberation of the libido', the first half of our century was demonstrably *not*

RIGHT: Table showing global assumptions on the relative amount of sexual activity in the various decades of life.

DECADE	RANKING FOR SEXUAL ACTIVITY
0–10	5
10–20	2
20–30	1
30–40	3
40–50	4
50–60	6
60–70	7
70–80	8
80–90	9
90–100	10

RIGHT: Table indicating probable ACTUAL ranking of relative sexual activity between human beings by decade.

DECADE	RANKING FOR SEXUAL ACTIVITY
0–10	10
10–20	5
20–30	3
30–40	4
40–50	6
50–60	2
60–70	1
70–80	7
80–90	8
90–100	9

liberated as far as its attitude towards both sex and sexual behaviour was concerned. For example, it was considered a revelation when the initial studies of Masters and Johnson revealed the fact that people over 40 actually, and regularly, enjoyed an active sex life.

What numerous studies are now revealing, including the later studies by Masters and Johnson and the Shere Hite Report – to mention but two of the more 'blockbuster' studies – is that the reality is very different from the assumption.

It increasingly appears that the actual ratings for sexual activity between consenting individuals are probably as shown in the above table.

'Impossible!' you might cry, '60–70 *can't* be No. 1!' Indeed, when these research findings were first made known at public seminars, the reaction of the audience was not only disbelief but often open derision.

The fact of the matter is, however, that when we investigate 'standard' day-to-day life, the popular assumptions become more unreasonable and the new survey findings far more understandable and reasonable.

SEXUAL ACTIVITY: THE EMERGING PICTURE

I. DECADE 20–30 (ACCORDING TO GLOBAL ASSUMPTIONS)

'Surely this *must* be the most active sexual decade?'

Certainly not 'surely'.

Consider the statistics and the operational facts of life for those in their twenties. The average couple is married at the age of 19 or 20. Within the first year of marriage, when there is usually considerable sexual activity, they also have to find regular employment, become accustomed to each other's habits and either rent or purchase accommodation.

Within the second year (they are now 21!), this 'average' couple will have their first child. Pressure of work and pressure of paying the bills begin to increase, and by the end of the year the woman is pregnant again. In the following year of their marriage the second child arrives. If ever there were an energy-draining, contraceptive device it is two young offspring.

For the rest of the decade, both mother and father are attending to the increasing demands of a growing young family and the accelerating sapping of all their resources, especially finances and time.

Sexual activity is not nearly so 'active' as is generally assumed.

2. DECADE 10–20

Far less sexual activity than is often supposed. For many children the pre-teen and early teen years are a continuation of the habit patterns of their first 10 years. Although the *thought* of sexual activity may take up increasing time, the *actual* activity is frequently limited. This is because:

☆ much contact is still 'public'
☆ fear of an unknown area of activity (pregnancy, disease, damage to reputation) inhibits that activity
☆ ignorance of the activity often leads to very brief contact
☆ roiling emotions of the teenage years often lead to hurt feelings and lengthy periods of abstinence
☆ in many societies and religions, sexual contact between minors is actively discouraged.

3. DECADE 30–40

During this decade work demands, and the demands on finance and time, continue to increase. And the children become *teenagers!* At this stage of their lives the parents are very like male and female birds in the latter stages of spring, who spend their entire day searching for and bringing home food to their screeching fledgelings. At the end of the day there is often hardly enough energy to crawl into bed, let alone make love in it!

Not a particularly active sexual decade.

4. DECADE 40–50

This decade, as generally predicted by those surveyed, is even less active than the previous one. This is *not* because of any genetical evolutionary imperative. It is entirely due to lack of opportunity, and the fact that enormous energy is being devoted to other areas of activity.

By this decade, the pressures of work are either increasingly demanding or increasingly crushing. If the individuals are continuing to progress in their professional careers, then they will often be required to work 14 to 16 hours a day, six to seven days a week, frequently sacrificing holidays along the way.

If the career has for some reason stalled or failed, then demotivation, dis-illusion and listlessness tend to set in, draining creativity, inspiration and sexual energy.

And children are often still present, having either moved on to higher edu-cation and all the financial and emotional strains that places upon the parents, or having lingered on in the family home to save themselves the financial bur-den of finding and paying for accommodation.

5. DECADE 0–10

Very little sexuality between individuals. This is obviously because the sexual chemicals have not 'kicked-in', because contact is normally limited to public 'arenas', and because societies do not as a rule encourage such behaviour.

A SEXUAL EBB TIDE?

6. DECADE 50–60

The fifties increasingly represent a turning-point in 'sexual decline'. With a growing number of organizations offering early retirement packages, 55 is becoming a not uncommon retirement age. Like a runner gaining energy from seeing the finishing line, the person who has worked for 30 years is often re-energized by the thought of their impending freedom.

When retirement at such an age does take place, a whole new world of opportunity arises. The point is poignantly made in the following story.

A couple who had married in their early twenties had worked their hearts and souls out raising a family, both taking on extra work to supplement their standard income. They had raised four children, each born two years apart. The parents had successfully put each child through school, and also through college and university.

The youngest child was about to enter her final year of university, immediately upon graduation going abroad for both travel and work experience. Because of the emotional significance of this last 'departure' from the family nest, the parents drove the girl back many hundreds of miles to her university and then spent a leisurely few days driving home.

As they entered their driveway, the wife turned to her husband, smiled broadly and said, 'Welcome, my darling, to the honeymoon home.'

Your imagination can fill in the sexual details of their lives up to and beyond that magical point in time.

7. DECADE 60–70

The new No. 1!

Why? Because at this time of life, in modern society, tens of millions of individuals are still exceptionally fit, both physically and mentally, are wealthy, curious and ready to enter, in the best sense of the word, their second childhood.

A remarkable confirmatory story for this decade of life is that of an Englishwoman whose husband had died in his early sixties. After mourning for a number of years, she asked her children whether they thought it appropriate if she began to search for a boyfriend. She explained that their father had been the only lover she had ever known, and that she seriously wanted to explore sexual life in the way that modern young girls did. Her children agreed that it would be a good idea, though little did they know what amazing stories were to follow.

In the space of three years this woman was approached by, and had love affairs with, a 50-year-old Hungarian, a 33-year-old Italian, a 62-year-old Englishman, a 24-year-old American football player, to mention just a few!

When she brought her latest 'new boyfriend' home for acceptance by the family, the usual roles became almost reversed, the children having to admonish the affectionate couple for consistently 'billing and cooing' in public, and for cuddling and fondling each other incessantly.

Opportunities to pursue lifelong dreams are increasingly available, and the chance to explore an intimate relationship with the person with whom you have lived a very 'public' family life is at last possible. Or, in a different scenario, the chance to explore a relationship with a new 'Significant Other' opens up numerous other avenues for exploration. A delightful story illustrates this point.

At a seminar given by Tony Buzan in the mid-1980s, he was lecturing on precisely the points covered in this survey of the decades. At the lunchtime break a magnificently fit 65-year-old lady rushed up to the stage, grabbed his hand vigorously and, with blazing eyes, said, 'Thank you! Thank you! Now I can go home and tell my lover that we are *not* both crazy!'

In addition to all these inviting characteristics and situations is the fact that by this time the individual is far more sexually experienced, considerate and aware. This means that love-making, instead of comprising the rushed physical urgencies of younger generations, can be a more drawn-out, exploratory, experimental and romantic affair.

8. DECADE 70–80

In contradiction to the standard stereotype, 70–80-year olds are often exceptionally vigorous, energetic and enthusiastic. As you read this sentence, many septuagenarians will be climbing mountains, running marathons, preparing for the Veterans' Olympics and making passionate love!

In addition to having amassed a wealth of experience, they have amassed massive capital. Economists estimate that over 70 per cent of the world's wealth is owned by those over 70.

With continued physical and mental vigour, and with vast resources at their disposal, this age group – still bursting with sexual energy – is active.

9. DECADE 80–90

Little research has been done on this age group. However, initial reports seem to indicate that there is no real change in either sexual desire or activity as people move from their seventies to their eighties.

Mae West, for example, kept a bevy of male lovers to satisfy her undimmed sexual desires throughout her later years. She said they kept her fit, happy, stimulated and fulfilled, her only complaint being that the younger ones lacked stamina.

This area is ripe for exploration, and the authors commend investigation of this area by the reader! Send us *your* stories!

10. DECADE 90–100

Stories such as the one that open this chapter abound: of 90-year-olds who are still exceptionally active in the sexual arena. The great Spanish artist Pablo Picasso was known to prowl the territory around his studios throughout his eighties and nineties in search of young lovers.

It appears that the twin flames of the human spirit and human sexuality burn brightly throughout life, and that the romantic impetus actually increases with age. It is incumbent on each one of us to nurture all three in ourselves and in others.

DERISION AND PREJUDICE

Why is it, when the facts are so apparent, rational and natural, that we can have got it all so dreadfully wrong? The answer lies in the fact that most modern nations have brought up children with the erroneous belief that their bodies are somehow dirty, that sex is somehow considered 'naughty', and that after the production of children, the function of sexuality is finished.

The sad irony is, therefore, that children grow up considering their parents to be somehow asexual, and incapable of imagining that their mother and father ever engaged in the very activity that brought them to life. This belief feeds upon itself, becoming a self-fulfilling prophesy that bridges the generation gap, seeding itself implacably into the future.

The Age Heresy, and this chapter in particular, is designed as an antidote to this global mental disease.

LOVE AS BRAIN FOOD

Further support for sex-throughout-life comes from the fields of brain and nutritional research.

It has been found that the brain requires four essential 'foods' for its survival. These are:

1. Oxygen
2. Biological nutrition
3. Information
4. Love

We all know that the brain must have material supplies for it to function, so oxygen and nutrition are clearly vital. What is frequently not realized is that information and love are a prerequisite for a healthy and active brain as you age. *Without these essential elements, the brain will go into decline and die.*

A simple thought-experiment will convince you of the importance of the vital thought-element, love. Think about the devastating *physical* effects you would experience, or have experienced, when the person whom you truly love convinces you, with a few powerful and well-chosen words, that they not only don't love you but are in fact totally indifferent to your existence. The brain *needs* love, and the physical touching and fondling that accompany it.

BRAIN FLASH

SLIMLINE RABBITS

An amusing incident in an experiment on nutrition and cholesterol-intake confirms the brain's need of love. American nutritionist William Glasser was feeding rabbits a diet that was particularly high in cholesterol. The purpose of the experiment was to determine appropriate cholesterol levels and to discover what levels would be dangerous — i.e., would cause unhealthy increases in weight.

The rabbits in the experiment lived in a number of communal cages and, after having been given various differing diets, were all put on the same high-cholesterol diet. All former variables were kept constant, and it was assumed that all the rabbits would react similarly.

Extraordinarily, all but one of the cages of rabbits performed as expected. The exception contained rabbits that were identical genetically to those in the other cages, yet for some inexplicable reason they remained sleek, slim and healthy while all the rabbits in the other cages gained weight as predicted. Glasser and his colleagues went into deep and extensive analysis, comparing blood samples, checking genetic codes, analysing the material of the cages, confirming that all environmental surroundings were indeed identical for all the rabbits, and reviewing their dietary records to look for anomalies. Every avenue of investigation was a dead-end.

Approximately a week later, with the 'slimline' rabbits maintaining their svelte condition against all predictions while consuming the high-cholesterol diet, one of the researchers happened, by chance, to be passing the research lab late at night, when he saw the light on. Going in to investigate, he found one of the night researchers holding one of the renegade rabbits. When asked what she was doing, she explained that the night-time shift often became very boring and, as a passionate lover of animals, and especially of rabbits, she would give herself regular breaks and simply come into the laboratory and spend five or ten minutes fondling and playing with the rabbits in this particular cage, to whom she had become attached. The experiment had provided a stunning result that no one had either planned for or expected. As Dr Glasser succinctly and wittily put it in his conclusion to the research:
'Eat what you like, but get a little loving every day.'

PHYSICAL HEALTH

Medical science is providing, on a daily basis, evidence that the human body can stay exceptionally fit and strong into its second century, if it is exercised appropriately and properly. The global misapprehension that, after your early twenties, everything sinks into an inevitable and rapid decline is being relegated to the dustbins of history.

A well-exercised body has a pint more blood than a poorly exercised one, with the blood providing a high-octane supply of oxygen to all the organs, especially the brain and the genitals. With a stronger heart beating more slowly and rhythmically, stress is reduced, confidence increased, all the organs enabled to function more efficiently, the risk of disease reduced, muscle tone improved, general alertness and energy levels raised, and stamina – physical, mental and sexual – greatly enhanced.

Throughout life, and especially to guarantee sexual longevity, the following three forms of physical toning should be undertaken approximately three times a week, for at least 20 minutes each:

1. AEROBICS

Aerobic training refers to the cardiovascular system, and is an exercise that keeps your heart beating at between 110 and 150 beats per minute. Excellent exercise to maintain this form of physical health includes swimming, the use of aerobic machines, cycling, rowing, dancing, running, very rapid walking and intense love-making.

2. FLEXIBILITY

Baby-like gymnastic flexibility can be maintained throughout a lifetime. Tony Buzan's 91-year-old neighbour, Tom Benning, who managed a farming estate for the bulk of his life, can, with a twinkle in his eye, lock his knees straight, raise his arms towards the sky and, bending at the hips, place his hands flat on the ground.

3. STRENGTH

Muscular strength can similarly be maintained throughout life. Excellent methods for maintaining muscular strength include weight-training, rowing, rapid swimming

> **BRAIN FLASH**
>
> *BE FLEXIBLY BODIED*
> *Excellent exercises to maintain lifelong flexibility include: yoga, stretching exercises, the Japanese martial art of Aikido, the Chinese martial art of Tai Chi, swimming, gymnastics, dance and flexibly-minded and flexibly-bodied love-making. The Indian bible of the art and science of love-making and sexuality, the* Kama Sutra, *is an excellent hand- (for want of a better word) book.*

and running, gymnastic dance, isometric training and the more athletic forms of love-making.

Is it worth doing all these? Yes, it is!

A body that radiates health and energy also radiates billions of sexual and other messages to every other person with whom it comes into contact. And your body is a far more complex and precious instrument than you may ever have thought. Look at the information below to find out just how incredible the human body is, to help you realize how vital it is that you maintain the fitness of your own body, and to help you understand that when you are exploring a loving and sexual relationship, you are exploring a miracle.

THE MIRACLE OF THE HUMAN BODY

If you are going to continue to develop throughout your life, what exactly is it that you are going to develop?

Consider the following staggering facts about the average human being, which means you.

1. Each human is created from a single sperm, one of 400 million produced by the father, and from a single egg produced by the mother. These eggs are so small that it would take two million to fill an acorn cup.
2. Within each sperm and egg combination there is the capacity to create about 300,000,000,000,000 billion humans. **All of them are unique.**
3. Each human eye contains 130 million light receptors.
4. Each human ear contains 24,000 fibres, which are able to detect enormous ranges and subtle distinctions in the molecular vibrations of the air.
5. To empower body movement, locomotion and environmental sensitivity, we have 200 intricately architectured bones, 500 totally co-ordinated muscles and 7 miles (11 km) of nerve fibres.
6. The human heart beats 36,000,000 times each year, pumping 600,000 gallons (2,727,600 litres) of blood each year through 60,000 miles (96,560 km) of tubing, arteries, veins and capillaries.

Science Photo Library

ABOVE: Leonardo da Vinci believed that 'Everything connects to everything else.' So by learning how your brain works, you stimulate it by association to perform better.

Bibliothèque des Beaux Arts, Paris/Giraudon/ Bridgeman Art Library London

ABOVE: Tempted by the Devil, Goethe's Faust agreed to forfeit his soul if he ever stopped striving and accepted a life of pure pleasure.

BELOW: Dr Marion Tinsley's greatest achievement was beating the Chinook draughts computer in London in 1992 when he was 65 years old.

Courtesy of The International Brain Club

Re-formatted by Lady Mary Tovey

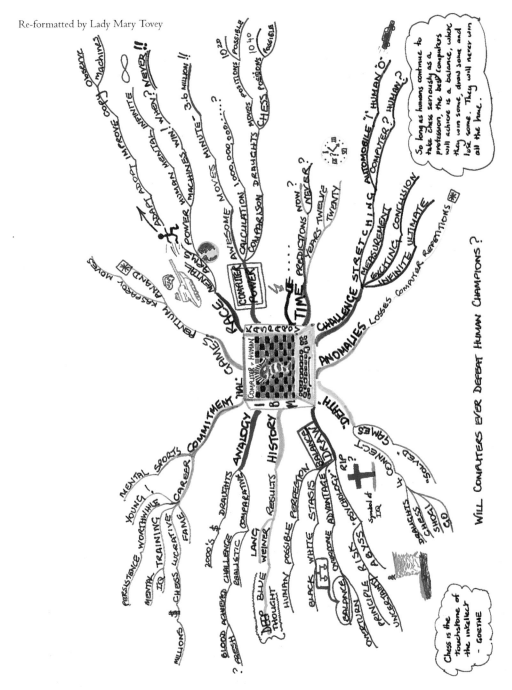

ABOVE: Ray Keene's lecture 'Will computers ever defeat human champions?' finished on time, to the nano-second, using this Mind Map.

Re-formatted by Lady Mary Tovey

DIET

14 DAYS

CUT OUT SUMPTUOUS FOOD!

GENERAL
- MAINTAIN ENERGY GOALS
- REDUCE POUNDS
- TWO WEEKS DURATION
- UNIMPORTANT!! AMOUNTS
- POACHED BOILED EGGS
- UNIMPORTANT DRINKS BLACK COFFEE
- ALL MEALS LEMON TEA

SUNDAY
- CHICKEN
- CABBAGE VEG TOMATOES
- HALF GRAPEFRUIT
- FRESH FRUIT SALAD LUNCH
- STEAK DINNER

SATURDAY
- TWO EGGS
- SALAD TOMATOES
- SPINACH LUNCH
- FISH DINNER
- CARROTS CABBAGE

FRIDAY
- TOAST
- HALF GRAPEFRUIT
- TWO EGGS LUNCH
- SPINACH DINNER

THURSDAY
- FRESH FRUIT SALAD LUNCH
- SHREDDED CABBAGE
- TWO EGGS TOAST DINNER

AVOID
- SUBSTITUTES FRYING SNACKS UNLISTED
- ALCOHOL SUGAR FAT OIL BUTTER DRESSINGS
- BREAKFAST STANDARD COFFEE
- GRAPEFRUIT HALF EGGS TWO

MONDAY
- LUNCH SALAD FRUIT FRESH
- DINNER EGGS SALAD GREEN GRAPEFRUIT HALF

TUESDAY
- LUNCH CHICKEN TOMATOES
- DINNER STEAK TOMATOES

WEDNESDAY
- LUNCH LAMBCHOP TWO TOMATOES SALAD
- DINNER EGGS SALAD OLIVES

TRIAL
EVENT
FEEDBACK
CHECK
ADJUST
SUCCESS!

ABOVE: *Ray Keene managed to lose two and a half stone (16kg) following this Mind Map for losing weight.*

7. Human lungs are composed of 600,000,000 globes of atmosphere-sensitive capacity.

8. The blood circulating within the human body contains 22 trillion blood cells. Within each blood cell there are millions of molecules, and within each individual molecule is an atom oscillating at more than 10 million times per second.

9. Two million blood cells die each second. These are replaced by two million more.

10. The human brain contains a billion neurones or nerve cells, which amounts to almost 200 times as many cells as there are people currently inhabiting the planet.

11. The human brain contains 1,000 trillion protein molecules.

12. Each human body has four million pain-sensitive structures.

13. Throughout the human body there are 500,000 touch detectors.

14. There are 200,000 temperature detectors in the body.

15. Within each human body there is enough atomic energy to build any of the world's greatest cities many times over.

16. Since the beginning of time there have been 70 billion humans, each one astoundingly different from all the others.

17. The human olfactory system, or sense of smell, can identify the chemical oderant of an object in one part per trillion of air.

THE BRAIN, SEX, LOVE AND ROMANCE

International journalist Nanci Hellmich recently surveyed top-selling romance writers to discuss the **qualities that were most sexually appealing** in heroes and heroines.

> ### BRAIN FLASH
>
> #### SEX AND THE BRAIN
> *Throughout your life your body is a potentially potent sexual force.*
>
> *You may be surprised and pleased to know that it carries a sexual organ that is easily the largest on Earth — not your genitals, but your brain! Sex is a physical and mental activity, with the mental side playing the far more powerful part. If you continue to develop your mental intelligence throughout life, especially your imaginative powers, you will be continuing to develop your sexual potency.*

The results will be particularly satisfying to those people who are continually striving to improve their mental performance as they age.

I. JUDY MCNAUGHT *(ALMOST HEAVEN)*:

IDEAL HERO: 'Strong, witty, intelligent. All my heroes are good communicators.'
IDEAL HEROINE: 'Very close to the hero. A sense of humour, intelligent.'

2. HEATHER GRAHAM POZZESSERE *(FORBIDDEN FIRE)*:

IDEAL HERO: 'Fun to be with, honest, bright.'
IDEAL HEROINE: 'Someone who definitely has a mind of her own. Intelligent, smart, willing to take chances.'

3. DONNA HILL *(ROOMS OF THE HEART)*:

IDEAL HERO: 'The man of your dreams, strong but can be gentle. Career-oriented.'
IDEAL HEROINE: 'She needs to be strong, determined. Someone who can handle both a career and love life. Intelligent, gentle, usually attractive.'

4. BEATRICE SMALL *(THE SPITFIRE)*:

IDEAL HERO: 'A man who is intelligent, willing to learn from a woman. A man who has a sense of humour.'
IDEAL HEROINE: 'I like a woman with a sense of humour. You need more than just a beautiful woman who responds to sexual overtures. She needs a brain.'

Surprisingly perhaps, the brain and intelligence came top of the sexual hit-parade.

As we showed in the life-expectancy chart in Chapter Two (see page 26), if you enjoy regular sex once or twice a week you can add two years to your standard life-expectancy, and you can also add another two years if your intelligence is above average (the average IQ is 100).

ATTITUDE (MIND-SET)

We can now see that sex-through-the-decades is not doomed to an inevitable decline. It is a field of endless opportunity, bounteous enjoyment, and infinite possibilities for learning and sharing human intimacies with others.

When you carry into the sexual arena – no matter what your age – a body that is beautifully fit, a mind that is intelligent, creative, agile and alert, and an attitude that is constantly curious, open, exploratory, childlike, romantic and concerned, then your sex life and partnerships will be ones of growing ecstasy.

WHAT SHOULD I DO NOW?

I. Simply one thing: keep it up!

CHAPTER EIGHT

MENS SANA IN CORPORE SANO

INTRODUCTION

In 'The Methuselah Mandate' we saw that the brain cell is the core of
any programme for development with age. We now set you, in this chapter, yet another challenge – to develop a comprehensive 'Good New Habit'
of overall and developing physi-
cal health. Only in this way can
the billion mini bio-computers
that are directing you operate at
their maximum capacity and multiply their potentially infinite
connections in the most effective
manner.

We explain the benefits of exercise and diet in living longer and
staying mentally and physically fit,
citing expert medical opinion. To
achieve a healthy mind *(mens sana)*
you must constantly strive to contain it within a healthy body *(in
corpore sano)*.

> ### BRAIN FLASH
>
> *A HARVARD STUDY SAYS: HARD EXERCISE
> WILL LEAD TO LONGER LIFE*
> *'Harried executives may shoehorn an occasional
> squash game or round of golf into their over-
> scheduled lives. Office clerks may sometimes trade a
> quick bite for a gym class during lunch hours. But
> if they want to get more out of their exercise
> routine than a competitive attitude or a leaner look,
> they are going to have to step up the pace.
> Researchers tracked 17,300 middle-aged men over
> 20 years and found those who exercised vigorously
> almost every day lived longer than those who broke
> a sweat only once or twice a week. Half-hearted
> huffing wasn't enough to make a difference, says
> Dr I-Min Lee, who led the study. It does not add
> years to your life.'*

FOOD FOR THOUGHT — AND EXERCISE, TOO

What you should eat, as life goes on, to maintain a peak of mental and physical stamina and energy is a vital topic. We decided to ask Dr Andrew Strigner, the Harley Street consultant physician with a special interest in nutrition and in improvement in one's use of the mind, for his direct personal advice. This is what he told us, exclusively for this book.

'I have always had an interest in nutrition. Sadly, when I began my medical education, I discovered that it was not part of the medical curriculum, the result being that I qualified feeling that I knew little more than my patients. Knowing one's own limitations, however, can stiffen one's resolve. So, continuing the search, I was fortunate to discover the McCarrison Society. Founded originally by a number of doctors, scientists and veterinary surgeons, it was devoted to the study of the relationship between nutrition and health and to the promulgation of this knowledge.

'Subsequently I discovered other researchers worldwide. What I found staggering is the amount of actual knowledge that exists, but which tends to remain with the researchers (some of whom appear not to know of the existence of others in the field) and is only slowly released. Curiously, much of this appears in the popular Press, perhaps in magazine articles, and is read by an increasingly interested lay public. They, in turn, are putting pressure on the medical profession, thereby causing the doctors to seek the answers.

'Happily, some of our newer medical schools, Oxford and Southampton among others, include nutrition on their curricula.

'The study of nutrition is the more fascinating because of the contributions made by people in other disciplines: epidemiologists, anthropologists, palaeoanthropologists, anatomists, physiologists, biochemists and, of course, clinicians.'

Nutrition is especially important for those who plan to have children at a later age.

HEALTH BEFORE CONCEPTION

Remember that each partner contributes genetic material to the embryo. The health of the father-to-be is as important, therefore, as that of the mother-to-be. It was, for example, long considered that Down's Syndrome resulted from the mother being too old to produce a healthy child. Evidence, backed by recent research reported in France, now indicates that many Down's Syndrome babies result from a defect in the father; most likely due to faulty nutrition, rather than to age.

HEALTH DURING PREGNANCY

Animal breeders and veterinary scientists have long known that good nutrition of the mature mother during pregnancy is vital, and have gone to considerable lengths to ensure it. Until recently the same attention has not been paid to human beings. It is now recognized that neural tube defects (i.e., lack of proper development of the brain and spinal cord) can be caused by deficiencies in the diet. In the UK lack of folic acid, one of the B vitamins, appears often to be the cause, while recent work in Dublin implicates also a deficiency of vitamin B_{12}. Other studies indicate that, in some Far Eastern countries, serious zinc deficiencies can produce similar defects.

A DIET FOR THE BRAIN

For a baby, milk is the most important brain food: milk, meaning human milk. To clarify this, let us give you an example.

At birth, a calf weighs 80–100 lb (36–45 kg), and at six months, suckling its mother, nearer to 500 lb (226 kg). In contrast, the human baby, born weighing 7–8 lb (3–4 kg), will weigh only about 14 lb (6 kg) at six months of age.

The difference arises from the fact that cows' milk contains a large amount of protein, for body-building, and considerable amounts of saturated fat, which provides the energy for growth. Human milk, on the other hand, contains much less protein, relatively little saturated fat, but large amounts of unsaturated fatty acids. Some of these, together with other substances called cerebrosides, are designed specifically for the construction of the brain and nerve tissue throughout the body. They are needed because the human brain continues to grow for about three years after birth, whereas the cow's brain hardly alters.

Put briefly, human milk builds big brains, whereas cows' milk makes big bodies.

A DIET FOR LIFE

The following recommendations, some of which may run contrary to contemporary opinion, are based on the most recently available dietary knowledge. Full explanations of every statement would require a complete book, so the explanatory notes are necessarily brief. A sound and enjoyable nutritional scheme for a longer and healthier life should include:

1. ANY KIND OF LEAN MEAT, especially wild or game meat (e.g. pheasant, partridge, grouse, rabbit , hare, venison), including offals such as liver and kidney. These, of course – apart from being highly enjoyable – provide protein, carbohydrate, water, minerals, some vitamins and, importantly, the omega-3 essential fatty acids. These are necessary for the renewal of cell-membranes, hormones, and for the transport of minerals throughout the body; also for the formation of many of the neuro-transmitters, which allow for proper brain and nerve function.

2. ANY KIND OF FISH, including the 'oily fish' – herring, mackerel, sardine, tuna, salmon, etc. The latter are also sources of omega-3 essential fatty acids. So much dietary advice is puritanical and offputting, but think about how much fun you can have with smoked salmon, oysters, lobsters, crabs and prawns!

3. AS MUCH VARIETY OF VEGETABLE AS POSSIBLE: leaf, stalk, root, pulse, fungus – mushrooms, broccoli, potatoes, cabbage, spinach, lettuce, peas, beans, onions, garlic, peppers... greens in general. These are all important sources

of different minerals, vitamins, fibre, and of another group of essential fatty acids, labelled omega-6.

4. OCCASIONAL EGGS (i.e., not every day, but perhaps 2–3 times weekly). The restriction is not because of the cholesterol content of eggs (which to a healthy person is insignificant) but because too-frequent consumption can produce an intolerance in some people. This would be a pity, as eggs are a valuable food for us.

5. MINIMAL SATURATED FAT (butter, dairy products, fatty meat from domesticated animals such as lamb, beef and pork) – although this cannot be eliminated totally, nor should it be. It carries some fat-soluble vitamins and provides texture and flavour, but its main value is as a concentrated source of energy. Anyone undertaking considerable regular physical effort (e.g. hewing coal, lumberjacking) or living in very low temperatures would require the fuel to meet their energy expenditure. Most of us do not.

6. FRUIT AND NUTS in moderation and in seasonal variety.

7. SUGAR, and processed foods, such as biscuits and cakes, to which sugar has been added, should, as far as possible, be omitted from the diet. Although the body uses sugar (glucose) as its main fuel, it prefers to produce its own from the food that we eat and to maintain carefully the correct levels. Too much sugar in the diet upsets this mechanism. Sugar is also one of the factors linked significantly to heart disease.

8. GRAINS (i.e., cereals, especially wheat-based products) should be used with moderation and great care. Rye bread can often be tolerated more readily than wheat.

9. MILK AND MILK PRODUCTS should, similarly, be used with caution.

In evolutionary terms, the last three items are relatively new to our diet and there is firm evidence to show that a significant proportion of people can develop an intolerance to milk and wheat proteins.

We are told that milk is needed for calcium: not true! Think fit. No animal takes milk after it leaves its mother, yet each develops bones and teeth. There is, in fact, calcium in almost all the foods that we eat, and more than an adequate amount would be provided in the scheme that we have outlined for you.

To emphasize the undoubted and powerful connection between proper nutrition and mental ability, we quote a letter from John Harris, a reader of Ray Keene's *Times* chess column:

'I was never very good at chess, but I played a lot and improved tremendously in a prison camp in the war in Kuching, Sarawak. We had an old chap called Poole, who was Blue Funnel's marine superintendent in Batavia, and he was good: he had played as one of 40 simultaneous players against one of the greats, world champion Alekhine, and was the only one to win his game. He taught me several basic principles to follow.

'It was at chess that I first noticed the signs of mental deterioration that resulted from our desperate shortage of food. Around the middle of 1944 I found I could no longer visualize moves as far ahead as I had once been able to, and this became progressive. Fortunately, nearly all, if not quite all, of one's mental faculties recovered, provided that the body did.'

An optimistic note of phoenix-like mental resurrection.

AEROBIC EXERCISE

Aerobic exercise increases the efficiency with which air is taken in and oxygen is transported around the body. All aerobics involve deep breathing and repetitive pumping movements of the arms and legs and, for maximum benefit, should be undertaken for at least 20 minutes three times a week. As with all exercise, however, this applies only to those in good physical condition, and if you are in the slightest doubt, or have any history of heart trouble, then consult your doctor or physician first.

There are many types of aerobic exercise, including brisk walking, jogging, cycling, dancing, skipping, swimming, squash, tennis, skating, cross-country skiing, slow long-distance running and circuit training with weights. Some of these (e.g. dancing, walking, jogging, swimming) also have a social element; or, if the very idea of exercise is anathema to you, what about a brisk walk with your favourite dog!

There are numerous ways of exercising at home or in the gym. Among the many exercise machines available, one good possibility is the Concept II Indoor Rower (also known as the Concept II Rowing Ergometer). Rowing provides a total body workout, exercising the heart, lungs and circulatory system – and at the same time shaping and toning the muscles of your legs, back, shoulders and stomach. The wide range of motion involved also improves and maintains your flexibility and, because rowing is an impact-free exercise, the joints are protected, too.

The Concept II Indoor Rower's unique and sturdy design allows the user to duplicate the motion of on-water rowing and benefit from a time-efficient, non-jarring workout. It has been widely used in the toughest environments – from busy health clubs to oil rigs, prisons to police forces, and even at NASA astronaut training centres.

The key to sustaining an effective exercise programme is feedback. Instant feedback on the Concept II's performance monitor includes an integrated heart-rate facility. You can monitor your pace, calorie expenditure, distance, target output level (watts), time and heart-rate. The performance monitor also includes a memory function, which allows you to review your workout when you have finished.

The Concept II Indoor Rower is widely available in gyms. Alternatively, it can be purchased (for approximately £800/$1,200) for home use. Up to one million people around the planet use it every day. Both co-authors own one, but we are not on the company payroll, nor do we own shares in the company!

For further details contact: Concept II Ltd, 4 Prince of Wales Court, Church Street, Old Basford, Notts NG6 OGA. Tel: 0115-942 1925, Fax: 0115-942 4684; or Concept II Inc., RRI Box 1100, Morrisville, Vermont 05661-9727, USA. Tel: 1-802-888 6333, Fax: 1-802-888 4791.

BRAIN FLASH

GOOD HEALTH IS WORKING OUT

'It looks like any other council-run leisure centre, but The Lagoon in Hailsham, West Sussex, seems more of a shrine. Government Ministers, doctors and academics from all over Britain have been there and marvelled at its curative powers.

Four years ago, GP David Hanraty began prescribing exercise sessions for his sickest patients at the centre. The results astonished him. An overweight, 67-year-old, hypertensive diabetic was able to come off the drugs he had been prescribed; after six months of exercise, he had no symptoms of diabetes at all. Not all the results were so dramatic, but all the participating patients felt significantly better — whether they had depression, coronary disease or cancer of the rectum.

Since then, 70 local GPs have started to prescribe exercise at The Lagoon and 3,000 patients have benefited.

A serious accident had left George Grew partially paralysed four years ago. His wife Phyliss had a bent back. The couple, who are in their seventies, both report feeling better and being able to move about more easily since they started swimming at the Hailsham centre.

Prescribed exercise has also worked wonders for people trying to stop smoking, for post-natal depression and for more chronic mental conditions. "I sent a patient of mine with schizophrenia down to the centre," says Dr Hanraty. "Now she's on much less medication and better able to manage her condition." How does it work? Dr Hanraty believes that exercise boosts self-esteem and stimulates the immune system.'

Remember: if you are trying to change and improve your diet, and/or trying to take up aerobic exercise for the first time, then our advice in Chapter Four on transforming a Big Bad Habit into a Good New Habit will be of paramount importance to you.

BRAIN FLASH

DRINK TANK — RAISE YOUR IQ

'Recent good news comes from Age and Ageing, which reports that the work of Dr Stephen Iliffe, of the Whittington Hospital, suggests that elderly male drinkers score better in intelligence tests than non-drinkers. The study also showed that more than 96 per cent of those observed kept within the strict drinking limits recommended by the British Medical Association, and that the rise in intelligence was thus related to moderate, "intelligent", intelligence-raising intake.'

This finding is entirely consistent with our conclusions about drinking intelligently, as seen in the life-expectancy chart in Chapter Two. According to this, heavy and non-drinkers score less well in terms of life-expectancy than moderate drinkers.

Now look at the table below, which advocates sensible drinking as an antidote to heart disease, which is, of course, one of the industrialized world's most prolific and widespread killers. This chart shows that, throughout Europe, the number of deaths from heart disease per 100,000 people declines in relative proportion to the amount of wine drunk *per capita* per year, up to a maximum of 15½ gallons (70 litres) of wine per annum.

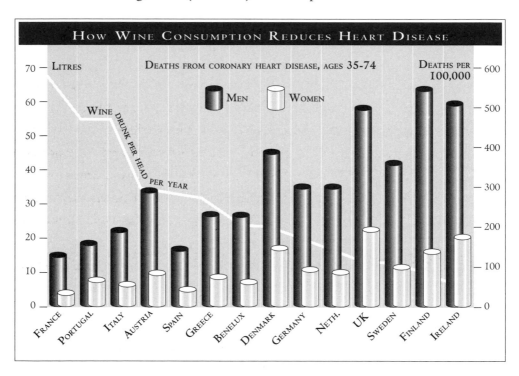

RAISE YOUR INTELLIGENCE, LOWER YOUR BLOOD PRESSURE: BUY A PET

Warwick Anderson, of the Baker Medical Research Institute in Melbourne, has produced the best evidence so far that pets are actually good for your mental (and physical) health. Anderson examined 5,741 people aged between

20 and 60 – 784 of whom were pet-owners – by offering them free health-risk evaluations.

Pet-owners turned out to be less stressed mentally, and to have significantly lower levels of cholesterol, as well as lower blood pressure. The results were similar across groups who dieted differently, or who were in different socio-economic categories.

James Serpell, of the Companion Animal Research Group at Cambridge, believes that the difference between the two groups is impressive and that it is **'stronger than improvements found in comparable studies on people who have switched to vegetarian diets or taken up exercise programmes'.**

PET POWER

This new research ties in with our life-expectancy chart in Chapter Two, which suggests that having close 'friends' increases your longevity. The companionship offered by a beloved pet may tie in with this. Stroking a pet is known to decrease stress and high blood pressure and to produce a general feeling of well-being – so much so that in some homes for the elderly it has been discovered that residents relax and cut down their intake of sleeping pills if a cat is present to be caressed and stroked. So want to

---

BRAIN FLASH

'VIRTUAL PETS'

'If they work too hard and their social life suffers, how about a little solace for the busy in the form of a hyper-sophisticated, computer-generated creature that's part dolphin, part bird? "Phink", an electronic pet, is the main inhabitant of Fujitsu's CD-ROM virtual world, called Teo. Sensors attached to a PC enable Phink to interact with humans in a social sense, courtesy of voice-analysis technology. Like a real pet, Phink can memorize faces and voices and perks up when its master calls. Soft tones ellicit a cuddlesome manner; hostile growling causes the image to fly away. Phink can also sing like a bird and learn new songs, as well as perform acrobatics. No bird seed is necessary. What about the possibility of other Phinks? Fujitsu is mum on many specifics of its project, but has suggested that a companion entity is somewhere in Teo and that the twosome will be able to propagate. So rewrite the song: "Birds do it, bees do it, even Phinks on their machines do it . . ."'

get fit, stay healthy, reduce stress levels and live a long life? Getting a pet could be the answer.

While recognizing the value of pets to a long and healthy life, some people (co-author Ray Keene among them) are highly allergic to certain animals (in his case cats). Technology, however, may have the answer (see 'Virtual pets' on page 101).

DA VINCI'S SLEEP FORMULA

Legend tells us that Leonardo da Vinci cat-napped for 15 minutes every four hours, giving him, for example, a total of an hour's extra sleep during a 16-hour working day.

According to Claudio Stampi, a researcher at the Institute of Circadian Physiology in Boston, Massachusetts, this unorthodox sleep schedule makes biological sense. Most animals, he says, naturally sleep this way.

During a three-week study, a graphic artist who adopted da Vinci's format enjoyed it so much that he volunteered for follow-up experiments. Additional studies of solo ocean-racers suggest that the contestants with the shortest sleep episodes do better than those who sleep for longer.

Where possible, and where appropriate, Stampi advocates that people should gently experiment with da Vinci's approach to sleeping.

It will be recalled that, in the life-expectancy chart, two years should be deducted from standard life-expectancy if you sleep for more than 10 hours consecutively on a regular basis.

WHAT SHOULD I DO NOW?

1. Improve your diet. Eat a regular substantial breakfast. Except on high days and holidays, avoid late-night blow-outs with alcohol.
2. Drink at least eight glasses of water a day. Herbal teas are highly recommended. Coffee and tea (non-herbal) are fine, but avoid sugar and be cautious if you feel you 'can't get by without them'.
3. Cows' milk, unseasonal fruit, grains and wheat-based products such as

pasta and bread are (evolutionarily) new additions to our regular diet. They can, therefore, often cause allergies. That is why you should be careful about consumption of them.

4. Take exercise regularly — at least three times a week for a period of from 10 minutes up to half an hour.

5. Take medical advice before embarking on a strenuous programme or if you want to exercise but suspect that you suffer from a physical weakness in any area.

6. Consider the following: brisk walking in a park, on a common or in the countryside (with a dog — if you have one); jogging; long-distance running; training for marathons; cross-country skiing; rowing; cycling; dancing; swimming and skating.

7. Join a tennis, swimming, martial arts or skating club, or a gym, to increase your circle of friends and your general social awareness.

8. Remember that 'petting' is good for people and pets.

9. Take cat-naps.

10. Notice the connection between what you eat and how your mind performs.

Your physiological and philosophical 'ducts' are now all in alignment. Your body should be becoming more healthy, and therefore you are ready to work specifically on developing your clarity and fluency of thought as you grow older, within the context of physiological and philosophical health. In order to do this it is *essential* that you find the right formulas for 'turning on' the gigantic generators of your mind. In the next chapter we reveal a 'secret weapon' that will allow you to do this — a tool that has become known as the Swiss Army knife of the brain.

CHAPTER NINE

MIND MAPS™: THE SECRET WEAPON

—

'TONY BUZAN'S INVENTION OF THE THOUGHT-ARRANGING PROCESS OF THE MIND MAP IS THE EQUIVALENT OF A THERMONUCLEAR DEVICE IN THE RACE FOR THE OLDER PERSON TO STAY AHEAD AND ALERT MENTALLY IN TERMS OF TAKING NOTES, PROBLEM-SOLVING, ORGANIZING YOUR THOUGHTS OR MAKING PRESENTATIONS.'

RAY KEENE

INTRODUCTION

This chapter concentrates on the improved organization of your thoughts and mental processes that can be brought about by using Tony Buzan's invention, the Mind Map. It specifically addresses in more detail the prob-

---

BRAIN FLASH

DIAGRAMS TRANSFORM THE WORLD OF ALGEBRA

'Simple pictures, rather than reams of bewildering calculations, could be the key to improving mathematics and physics teaching.

A study of great scientists, such as Sir Isaac Newton, has found that they used myriad sketches to uncover the laws of physics. Today's students have to plough through masses of algebraic problems. Many are left with scant understanding of the underlying reality, and it is thought that unenthusiastic and mediocre graduates in such fields as astronomy and engineering are the result.

Researchers have harnessed the picture-book approach of scientific geniuses into a computer system which might inspire students to greater things. It reveals to them the Laws of Motion and of the Conservation of Momentum and Energy, using moving diagrams.

Dr Peter Cheng, a psychologist at the Economic and Social Research Council's Centre for Development, Instruction and Training in Nottingham said: "The system allows you to draw diagrams using geometric shapes to find the answers to problems. They make the algebra come alive."'

---

lems outlined in Chapter Three – namely, the top 20 areas of mental performance requiring improvement among 40–50-year-olds.

It shows how adopting Mind Mapping techniques in your business, in everyday life, in presentations, even in making personal 'to do' lists, can combat the disorganized thinking that is often mistaken for the symptoms of encroaching old age and mental decline.

MIND MAPPING

'If you work in a business, academic, service or industrial environment, you will find Mind Mapping invaluable. When I was invited to lecture at the Royal Institution, London, in March 1995 on whether chess computers will ever defeat human world champions, I made the presentation, which had to last 60 minutes precisely – no more and no less – from a Mind Map. It worked to the nano-second, and afterwards I was most gratified when the academics and professors of the institute crowded around the podium to wonder at this new form of lecture notes.'

RAY KEENE

Tony Buzan now recounts the genesis of his revolutionary Mind Mapping concept.

THE GENESIS OF MIND MAPPING

The first major step occurred when I was 14. I was given numerous tests on intelligence, reading speed and memory and was told that I would never be able to change the results. As well as infuriating me, this was difficult for me to understand. **After all, physical exercise makes you stronger, so why should the right kind of mental exercise not improve your mental performance, too?** I immediately began to work on this problem and quickly realized that if I had the right technique, then my results would surely improve. It was at this stage that I also realized that the least productive method of trying to understand a subject was to take the kind of notes my teachers and lecturers standardly expected. I found them boring and worthless, and the more I took, the less I seemed to understand the material.

At the age of 20, while I was studying at the University of British Columbia, I began to work seriously on improving my memory and note-taking. This work developed into two branches.

1. I studied the nature of memory, and especially that which is recalled. This inevitably includes imagery and association.

2. **I studied the note-taking methods of the great brains and observed that, without exception, they all used images, pictures, arrows and other connective devices, while those who did less well in academic studies made only linear notes.**

The result of this combined study was the evolution of the concept of Mind Mapping. The more I discovered, the more excited I became. I felt like the discoverers of Tutankhamun's tomb. First of all, I had peered through a keyhole and seen the vague shapes of what might be fantastic artefacts. Then, I had entered the barely lit room and witnessed the incredible potential of its contents. Finally, I had managed to cast light on the wealth of treasure I had discovered.

I wanted very much to tell the world about my discovery, and I still do. The first communication of it came with publication of my *Use Your Head* book and the BBC television series of the same name, which was repeated every year for ten years. Major dissemination of the idea involved 15 years of worldwide travelling on lecture tours to academic, business and government institutions. Then, at the beginning of the 1990s, came the establishment, by Vanda North, of the Buzan Centres, where Radiant-Thinking Instructors are trained in these educational methods.

The Mind Map is a powerful graphic technique, which provides a universal key to unlocking the potential of the brain. It harnesses the full range of cortical skills — word, image, number, logic, rhythm, colour and spatial awareness — in a single, uniquely powerful manner. In so doing, it gives you the freedom to roam the infinite expanses of your brain. The Mind Map can be applied to every aspect of life where improved learning and clearer thinking will enhance your performance. Mind Maps are now used by millions of people around the world, from the ages of 5 to 105, whenever they wish to use their brains more efficiently.

Like a road map, a Mind Map will:

1. Give you an overview of a large subject/area.
2. Enable you to plan routes/make choices.
3. Let you know where you are going, and where you have been.
4. Gather and hold large amounts of data.
5. Encourage both daydreaming and problem-solving by looking for creative pathways.
6. Be extremely efficient.
7. Be enjoyable to look at, read, muse over and remember.

MIND MAP LAWS

1. Start to draw in the centre of a blank, unlined page of paper, with an image of the desired topic, using at least three colours.
2. Use images, symbols, codes and dimension throughout your Mind Map.
3. Select key words and print — using capitals or lower-case letters.
4. Each word/image must be alone and on its own line.
5. The lines must be connected, starting from the central image. In the centre, the lines are thicker, organic and flowing, becoming thinner as they radiate outwards.
6. Make the lines the same length as the word/image.
7. Use colours — your own code — throughout the Mind Map.
8. Develop your own personal style of Mind Mapping.
9. Use emphasis and show associations between different related topics in your Mind Map.

10. Keep the Mind Map clear by using numerical order or outlines to surround your branches.

How to Mind Map

1. Place a large white sheet of paper horizontally, or use a Mind Map pad.

2. Gather a selection of coloured pens, ranging from thin nib to highlighter.

3. Select the topic, problem or subject to be Mind Mapped. This will be the basis of your central image.

4. Gather any materials, research or additional information that is needed, so that you have all the facts at your fingertips. Now start to draw in the centre of your page.

5. Start with an image approximately 2½ in (3 cm) high and wide for A4 paper, and 4 in (10 cm) for A3.

6. Use dimension, expression and at least three colours in the central image in order to attract attention and aid memory.

7. Make the branches closest to the centre thick, attached to the image and 'wavy' (organic). Place the Basic Ordering Ideas (BOIs) or chapter headings on those branches.

8. Branch thinner lines off the end of the appropriate BOI to hold supporting data.

9. Use images wherever possible.

10. The image or word should always sit on a line of the same length.

11. Use colours as your own special code to show people, topics, themes, dates and to make the Mind Map more attractive.

12. Capture all your ideas, or those that others have contributed, then edit, reorganize, make more beautiful, elaborate, or clarify as a second and more advanced stage of thinking.

WHAT SHOULD I DO NOW?

Look at the uses and benefits of Mind Maps, which are clearly set out for you opposite.

Uses	Benefits
1. Learning	Reduce those 'tons of work', feel good about study, review and exams. Have confidence in your learning abilities.
2. Overviewing	See the whole picture, the global overview, at once. Understand the links and connections.
3. Concentrating	Focus on the task for better results.
4. Memorizing	Easy recall. 'See' the information in your mind's eye.
5. Organizing	Parties, holidays, projects, etc. **Make it make sense to you.**
6. Presenting	Speeches become clear, relaxed and alive. You can be at your best.
7. Communicating	Communicate in all forms with clarity and conciseness.
8. Planning	Orchestrate all aspects, from beginning to end, on one piece of paper.
9. Meetings	From planning to agenda, chairing, taking the minutes… these jobs can be completed with speed and efficiency.
10. Training	From preparation to presentation, make the job easier.
11. Thinking	The Mind Map will become a concrete record of your thoughts at any stage of the process.
12. Negotiating	All the issues, your position and manoeuvrability on one sheet.
13. Brain-blooming	The new brain-storming, in which more thoughts are generated and appropriately assessed. It is often assumed that the greater the quantity of ideas generated, the more the quality declines. In fact, the reverse is true. **The more you generate ideas and the greater the quantity, the more the quality increases.** This is a key lesson in understanding the nature of your own creativity.
14. Lectures	When you attend a lecture, use a Mind Map to keep a vivid visual memento of it.

If you look closely at all the above uses of Mind Maps you will see that they clearly, cogently and powerfully address certain problems of mental performance. Indeed, they address the top 20 concerns about mental performance expressed by the 40–50-plus age group of executives, business leaders and attendees at Tony Buzan's lectures.

CHAPTER TEN

THE EINSTEIN EQUATION: A NEW CHALLENGE

'E = MC²'

<small>ALBERT EINSTEIN</small>

INTRODUCTION

Now that you have learnt how to use the ultimate mental tool, let's turn to examples of some of the great geniuses who, at the age of between 40 and 90, exhibited the full range of mental qualities necessary for the expression of genius throughout life. Albert Einstein is the archetypal example.

Later in this chapter we provide a self-challenging chart of the qualities you need to develop in order to manifest your own burgeoning intelligence.

THE GENIUS QUEST

The ultimate mental accolade is to be regarded as a genius. We now comment on some of the key qualities that have led to such recognition. Simultaneously this section of the book poses you a fresh challenge: Can you train yourself to emulate these qualities, Goethe-style?

Our definition of genius encompasses many features that the great minds have in abundance. Among them are mental

---

> ### BRAIN FLASH
>
> *THE NATURE OF GENIUS*
> *Some commonly held theories about genius and creativity — that people are 'born' geniuses, or that it is a 'gift from God' — are a myth.*
>
> *Shortly before his death, Albert Einstein admitted, 'I know quite certainly that I myself have no special talent. Curiosity, obsession and dogged endurance, combined with self-criticism, have brought me my ideas.' And the inventor Thomas Edison echoes this notion: 'Godlike genius — godlike nothing! Sticking to it is the genius.'*

and physical strength — even those geniuses who are physically handicapped find the strength to fulfil their vision and goals. The Cambridge physicist Stephen Hawking, for example, should, according to medical opinion, have died 20 years ago. Instead, he is still very much alive and actively working, continuing to emulate Newton and Einstein in the depth of his revelations about science.

The definition of genius goes on to include recognition of the truth — many people waste energy pursuing false theories or ideas. It also includes: a love of the task; faith, vision, desire, commitment, planning; the ability to bounce back from mistakes; subject knowledge; a positive mental attitude; imagination; courage; and energy. Compare these with the qualities of the brain champions given in Chapter Six.

One of the most extraordinary examples of mental achievement that we ever witnessed came when we saw Dominic O'Brien in action at the Memoriad in 1993. Among numerous other feats, he recalled 100 spoken digits (read out at a rate of one every two seconds) perfectly on two occasions. When we first saw him do this we were shocked — we had never seen anything like it and, intellectually, we found it quite difficult to accept that it was possible. We had seen brilliant chess players, such as Kasparov, producing phenomenal combinations, but what Dominic O'Brien achieved equalled any of these. In the first Memoriad in 1991 he had achieved some impressive results, but now he was suddenly remembering something like 1,000 written digits, when previously it had been 200, or 15 packs of cards in one hour, instead of two. When we first saw it done we found it totally awesome, and still do.

Historically speaking, there are many achievements by many different people that have struck us. Here are just a few examples:

GERONTOLOGICAL MARVEL

We were deeply impressed by Michelangelo's achievement in beginning construction on the Dome of St Peter's in Rome at the age of 63, a task that he continued with utter dedication until the age of 89. The Pope commissioned him to undertake the task and, rather than whingeing about being too old or too tired, Michelangelo simply got on with it and produced one of the most brilliant works of art and architecture in history.

To the Ends of the Earth

A fact that is not often appreciated about the explorer Christopher Columbus is that he was the first voyager to risk striking directly away from the coastline. All previous explorers were terrified that they might lose their way back, or fall off the edge of the Earth. No one, therefore, had ever directly crossed the Atlantic Ocean from Europe to locate a new continent previously unknown to them. The only possible precedent was set by Polynesian seafarers, who did branch out but tended to hop from island to island, rather than sail out into the ocean at right-angles to the coast. Columbus's great navigational insight was that the trade winds worked in both directions, so he was confident that he had a means to return to his base. **Columbus was 41 years old when he set off on the world's first transatlantic voyage.**

Blind Zizka

Zizka, a particular hero of Ray Keene's, was a Bohemian general from the fifteenth century, who fought for the English at Agincourt against the French.

> ### BRAIN FLASH
>
> *Synapses-Increasers*
> *'Both Albert Einstein and Winston Churchill probably increased their synapses like crazy by practising art forms that seemed to have little to do with their everyday lives. Einstein played the violin, while Churchill painted landscapes.'*

He lost an eye in a later battle, thus rendering him completely blind, as he had already lost the other one in an earlier campaign. **Nevertheless, at the age of 51, he went on to win 12 major battles against the Holy Roman Empire,** usually against the most extraordinary odds. His forces (which often consisted of untrained peasants) would typically be outnumbered about 10 to 1 by the opposing army and yet emerged victorious time after time. He had immense energy and was stopped in his tracks only when he caught the plague and died. When we realize that, even by 1900, the average life-expectancy in Europe was only 50, his was quite an achievement.

KEEPING A MILITARY MACHINE UNCERTAIN

Werner Heisenberg was a physicist who was responsible for the discovery of the Uncertainty Principle. Loosely speaking, this states that you can never quite pin down atomic particles, because, as your knowledge of their position improves, there is a corresponding decrease in your knowledge of their momentum. His insight was to realize that this was not just some weakness in the experimental apparatus or the mathematics, but a fundamental law of nature.

This was brilliant enough in itself, but what also struck us about Heisenberg was the role that he played during the development of atomic weapons during the Second World War. He was, at the age of 40, Germany's leading expert on nuclear physics, but his work had been dismissed by the regime. When they realized, however, that he would probably be able to help them build an atomic bomb, the authorities changed their tune. Although aware that the project was perfectly feasible, Heisenberg managed to persuade them that it could not work, citing all sorts of technical and practical difficulties. His elaborate deception continued for about four years but, had it not worked, the outcome of the Second World War might have been very different.

There is no single (or simple) intellectual telltale sign of genius, such as linguistic or mathematical ability, but what the above examples all demonstrate is amazing persistence in an effort to achieve their vision. They were all highly focused on their goals, and all other factors became subordinated to this. Motivation is a key factor in the definition of genius. All the geniuses we have researched were totally motivated. Another recurrent trend is that they treat the whole planet as one gigantic IQ test and relish accepting the challenges thrown at them.

How to Make the Most of Your Mental Abilities

Decide what it is you want to do, and how important it is to you, and then determine if you are sufficiently motivated to carry it through to its conclusion. **You cannot get this knowledge from others – you must decide for yourself.** We are often, however, not sure what *is* really important to us, so we think making a list is a good idea. **An even better idea, as you will probably have realized by now, is to make a colour Mind Map of your priorities. Map out all the things that interest you and then rate them in terms of how important they are to you.**

You may, for instance, decide that you want to increase your income and thus concentrate on finding a new job, or on becoming better rewarded for the one that you do. Alternatively, you may decide that the most important thing for you is to enjoy your holidays more, so you may learn a new language or explore a foreign culture, which would have the by-product of being mentally stimulating. The possibilities are endless and will, of course, differ from person to person, but **the key factor is motivation.** If you are motivated enough to do what you want to do, then everything else will fall into place. People who are not motivated are unfocused and unable to concentrate their energies effectively.

What the Geniuses Can Teach Us

Successful achievement does not materialize out of nothing – it requires planning, plus a tremendous amount of hard work. Admiration for your peers and a desire to emulate them is another important factor. Many artistic careers are fashioned along the following logical lines: 'I want to become a great artist. X and Y are great artists whose work I admire. I will, therefore, study the lives of X and Y and try to emulate them.' Machiavelli talks about the importance of emulation in his book *The Prince.* If you are inspired, you copy and then surpass. If you aren't inspired, then you can't achieve anything. Cynicism is the enemy of genius.

THE SELF-CHALLENGING CHART

Dominic O'Brien selected memory as his field. Here is our selection of mental and physical skill areas that you might wish to take up as suggestions for personal challenges to enhance your life as you mature.

1. Mind Mapping
2. Learning and study (e.g. history, philosophy)
3. Memorizing
4. Speed-reading
5. Creative thinking
6. Intelligence – IQ
7. Mathematics, science, astronomy
8. The Arts (e.g. music, dance, painting)
9. Physical skills and sports
10. Vocabulary/language
11. Presenting/communicating
12. Personality development
13. Games and mind sports (e.g. chess, draughts, bridge, 'Go', 'Scrabble')
14. Martial arts (e.g. aikido)
15. Travel (exploring, mountaineering)

Once you have examined these, you can then prioritize items by highlighting the new skills that particularly interest you, listing them in the order you decide to work on them:

1. _____
2. _____
3. _____
4. _____
5. _____

Even better, map them out on a Mind Map.

Then monitor your changes and improvements over the years. Observe yourself getting better! To assist you in your endeavours, many activities have official assessment levels, by which you can objectively gauge your own performance. Chess federations, for example, regularly publish sanctioned ranking lists; organized martial arts clubs have their 'belt' and 'dan' systems; while the authors of this book have instituted a title and rating system for memory performance; and so on…

Write to or join the International Brain Club (for address see page 175) if you want to know, for instance, how to contact a Mind Mapping, memorizing, mind sports or martial arts group, society or association.

EXPANDING FRONTIERS

As our knowledge expands and we come to know more about the planet and the universe, so our opportunities also expand. We now know that human potential is virtually limitless and that, as knowledge increases, so does our mental capacity to absorb it. So, apart from the possibilities of shining in a particular field, we can also enjoy the attraction of becoming polymaths, as Leonardo, Michelangelo and Goethe were.

The capacity to turn negatives into positives is another excellent indicator of genius. This is not merely a case of fighting through adversity, but implies a conscious decision to look for the positives in what appear to be the most appalling circumstances.

Jose Luis Borges, the Argentinean writer, for example, had gone blind by his mid-fifties but, having done so, he then learnt Anglo-Saxon, which greatly enriched his life. And we have already observed the inspirational examples of Hawking and Zizka.

This is a recurring theme. Many of the geniuses of history are great survivors, who have suffered the most dreadful calamities but have refused to look at them negatively.

On a lighter note, we are great fans of the *Star Trek* series. In many episodes the *Enterprise* and its crew find themselves in some appalling situation and the only solution is to think their way out of trouble. As Spock once says, when he has become fatally irradiated: 'There are always possibilities.'

WHAT SHOULD I DO NOW?

1. Pick a genius (or geniuses) of particular interest to you. It could be Leonardo da Vinci, for his versatility; Beethoven, for his determination and heroism in the face of encroaching deafness; Columbus, for his courage and conviction.
2. Mind Map the qualities of your chosen genius(es).
3. Apply the lessons to your own life.
4. Pick one or more skills from the chart on page 115 and pledge yourself to become an expert in that area or areas. Start by Mind Mapping your chosen approach.

CHAPTER ELEVEN

THE GOLDEN PILGRIMAGE

———

'THE MASTERY OF SOME SIMPLE MNEMONIC SYSTEM MAY LEAD SOME PEOPLE TO REALIZE, FOR THE FIRST TIME, THAT THEY CAN CONTROL AND MODIFY THEIR OWN MENTAL PROCESSES.'

HANS EYSENCK, EXPERT ON IQ

INTRODUCTION

In this chapter we address one of the most pervasive and destructive delusions that the human race has so far devised: namely, that as the human brain gets older it degenerates, losing brain cells and experiencing rapid decline in the intellectual areas of memory, creativity, mathematics and linguistics.

In previous chapters we have provided increasing evidence that this is not the case. Now we bang the last nail into the coffin of what is, in fact, a ludicrously fallacious idea. Failing memory is, perhaps, the chief mental problem lamented by *everyone*. But memory loss as we get older is *not* inevitable, *not* necessary and certainly *not* true.

We now show you how to acquire and learn simple memory techniques (nothing too technical) and give further inspirational examples, this time of memory performance.

MEMORY

In *The Age Heresy* we define 'memory' not as a passive recorder of everyday data – pleasant or unpleasant – but as an active, focused laser-beam of the mind, in the fight to stay ahead mentally. If you train your memory (and we have already observed the dynamic influence that Mind Mapping can exert in this respect), the data will be at your fingertips to conquer new areas of subject knowledge, to run your organization more efficiently, to make more effective presentations... In short, to be increasingly decisive and creative. This chapter recounts key historical moments in the devel-

> ### BRAIN FLASH
> #### OLD DOGS ...
> '... old dogs rarely have real difficulty learning new tricks; they more often have difficulty convincing themselves that it is worth the effort.'

opment of memory techniques and portrays some awe-inspiring memory feats to stimulate your own achievements.

First, we take a look at the hard scientific evidence, showing that memory powers do not alter significantly at any age, as long as you continue to use your abilities and do not let them atrophy.

SCIENTIFIC EVIDENCE ON MEMORY LOSS WITH AGE – OR OTHERWISE

Memory loss associated with age may be more a reflection of how we view older people, how they view themselves and how we test them in the laboratory than of actual memory decline due solely to the ageing process. While test results do often reveal poor memory performance in the elderly, two factors that have been shown to confound these results are: level of interest and the use of timed performance.

Richard Reystak, in his book *The Mind* (1988), spent a great part of his chapter on ageing stressing that we do see a decrease in speed of processing in the elderly. However, there are mitigating factors, which are often overlooked or underestimated. Frequently in laboratory tests the elderly subject is not allowed adequate time in which to encode and recall information. Reystak points out that if elderly subjects are allotted as much time as they need, then they often perform at a level that is comparable with younger subjects in terms of recall. And D.A.Walsh points out that the level of interest can affect the performance of recall. He reports a study by B. Hulicka in which she tried to teach associations of actual words paired with nonsense letters. She found that many elderly subjects performed poorly because they refused to learn nonsense words, and felt that the task was not 'worth the effort'. When the task was changed to an association of occupational names paired with actual surnames, the elderly performed better. Walsh stresses that laboratory experiments may often be perceived as meaningless and may negatively affect the elderly subjects' performance, while making the task meaningful may positively affect their performance.

One important area of concern is that of neuronal loss due to normal ageing. There is no conclusive evidence regarding just how much of the brain is lost with age, and just what areas are affected. The interest regarding neuronal loss may, however, be misdirected. Reystak raises some major theoretical issues that are particularly relevant here. He reports on a study in which the amount of blood flow to, and oxygen consumption in, the brain were compared in healthy 20-year-old men and healthy 70-year-old men. *If* there is substantial neuronal loss, there should also be a decrease in blood flow and oxygen consumption. **The results showed that there was no difference between the groups on these measures.**

REDUNDANCY AND PLASTICITY

Reystak also points out that, even if there were neuronal loss accompanying the ageing process, the loss may be offset by the redundancy and plasticity of the brain.

Redundancy implies that there is a greater than necessary number of neurones in the brain, to the extent that neurones may die, with no reduction in observed behaviour. For instance, we may damage an area of the brain and still show little or no change in our behaviour. Plasticity refers to the fact that the brain can change in its organization. An area of the brain responsible for a particular function may be damaged, for example, with the result that another area of the brain may take over the function of the damaged area. In this way, as Reystak observes, neuronal cell loss due to normal ageing may, in fact, lead to greater functioning and more numerous connections in the remaining cells. This suggests that continually 'using' the brain (i.e., making more associa-

Library of Congress, Washington D.C/Bridgeman Art Library London

ABOVE: at the age of 41, Columbus set a precedent by striking out at right-angles to the shoreline in his bid to discover the New World.

RIGHT: In his eighties, Sophocles outwitted his son in court by reciting his latest tragedy verbatim.

Louvre, Paris/ Bridgeman Art Library, London

Scrovegni (Arena) Chapel, Padua/Bridgeman Art Library, London

ABOVE: Giotto's paintings in the Arena Chapel in Padua are structured as a memory theatre, using depth and perspective to make the images more memorable.

RIGHT: Toscanini's memory was proverbial: he regularly conducted without a score, and on one occasion wrote out an entire score from memory.

BELOW: Dominic O'Brien has three times won the World Memory Championship and his feats continue to astound.

Private Collection/ Bridgeman Art Library, London

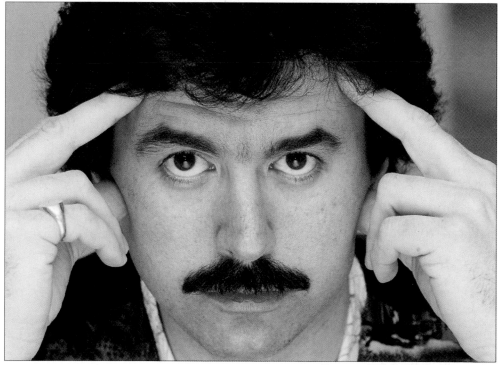

Courtesy of The International Brain Club

M. Defrisco/Allsport

Andre Camara/Times Newspapers Limited

During the past 40 years older generations have shattered physical world records. Bill O'Connor (main picture) has completed every London marathon since the first race in 1981.

Al Bello/Allsport

tions) can offset any naturally occurring loss due to cell death. This 'use it or lose it' idea is one that we emphasize throughout *The Age Heresy*.

OF RATS AND RESPONSIBILITY

There is a great deal of literature showing the effect on its subsequent development of using the brain. One interesting study is rather amusing. A. Greenough (cited in Reystak's book) trained rats to reach with a particular paw for pieces of chocolate-chip cookies. Later examination of the area of the brain responsible for motor movement revealed more synaptic connections compared to the brains of untrained rats.

Research also suggests that environment plays a critical role in human development. K.W. Schaie (cited by Reystak) conducted a 20-year study of 4,000 people and found that elderly people who maintained active social lives, took on social responsibilities and accepted new challenges outperformed those who led restricted lives. And by providing mental exercises utilizing spatial, numerical and verbal skills, Schaie induced over half of a group of elderly volunteers to improve their performance. He further suggests that memory in the elderly can be improved by the use of mnemonics.

One interesting study describing the use of mnemonics in the elderly was conducted by gerontologists E.A. Robertson-Tchabo, C.P. Hausman and D. Arenberg in 1982. In the first phase of the study, elderly subjects were given a list of words to memorize and recall. As expected, initial recall was low. The subjects were then given instruction on how to use a particular mnemonic while learning lists. Recall for the lists studied, using mnemonics, increased significantly. Days later, however, when they were required to learn and recall a list, performance was again poor. It appeared that the subjects did not spontaneously use the mnemonic technique to help them remember the final list.

In the second phase of the experiment, elderly subjects were divided into three groups, all of which were required to master a mnemonic technique and apply it to the list learnt in the training sessions. During the following test session, subjects in all three groups were required to memorize and recall a list of words. The subjects in Group 1 were instructed to 'use the method we have been using for the past few days'. The subjects in Group 2 were instructed to form the associations of the mnemonics and to describe verbally the images. The subjects in Group 3 were never instructed to apply the mnemonic techniques they had studied.

The results showed that the subjects in Group 3 recalled fewer words than those in Groups 1 and 2. Interestingly, there was no difference in performance between the subjects in Group 1 and Group 2. This suggests that mnemonics are valuable aids to memory, but that people need to learn how to develop and use them.

No Memory Loss – But Use It or Lose It

This information supports the belief that your memory need not diminish with increasing age. 'Use it or lose it' perfectly describes the conclusions reached in scientific literature. By practising and expanding your mental activ-

---

BRAIN FLASH

MIND SPORTS RECEIVE GRAND MASTER STATUS

The mental sport of memory testing and performance has become only the second in the history of mind sports to receive royal sanction for the award of Grand Master titles. The first mind sport to be so honoured was chess, when Tsar Nicholas II at the St Petersburg tournament of 1914 awarded the original chess Grand Master titles to the five chess greats, Lasker, Capablanca, Alekhine, Tarrasch and Marshall.

At a formal ceremony organized by the Brain Trust charity on 26 October 1995 at Hanbury Manor in Ware, Hertfordshire, Prince Philip of Liechtenstein sanctioned the initial award of Grand Masters of memory to, among others, Dominic O'Brien and his great rival Jonathan Hancock. These are the only two who have so far won the World Memory Championship.

The memory symbol, designed especially for the occasion, combines three elements: the Hippocampus, that part of the brain that is responsible for memory; the Knight's Head, over a background globe, linking it through chess to other mind sports worldwide; finally, the Horsehead Nebula, which is itself a memory trace, an image of that which transpired in the universe many millions of years ago but is still visible to us.

---

ities you can develop new connections and associations throughout your lifetime. **This finding is extremely relevant to you and your business.** All too often 'seniors' in the business place are seen as incompetent, because they can't perform as quickly as younger people. **However, they have a wider range of experience and association than younger, less experienced personnel, and their potential contribution is invaluable.** It is critical constantly to challenge your own mind and the minds of your co-workers, to strive to engage people and keep them involved, and to allow extra time for the elderly. Keep in mind that they are capable of 'learning new tricks', provided that they see its relevance, perceive it as worth while *and* feel motivated.

THE DISCOVERY OF THE RULES OF MEMORY

In his Rhône-Poulenc Science Book of the Year award-winning treatise *The Making of Memory: from molecules to mind*, Professor Steven Rose narrates the discovery of the rules of memory by a poet called Simonides, who lived around 477 BC.

Simonides' story first appears in *De Oratore* by the Roman writer and politician Cicero, who relates how Simonides was commissioned to recite a lyric poem in honour of the host of a banquet, the Thessalonian nobleman Scopas. The poem also, however, contained praise for the twin gods Castor and Pollux, which displeased Scopas so much that he would pay Simonides only half his fee, suggesting that the other half be collected from the gods. Later in the banquet Simonides received a message that two people were waiting to see him and, just after he left the hall, the roof collapsed, killing everyone there and mangling the corpses into an unidentifiable state. The two young men who had summoned Simonides were, of course, Castor and Pollux, taking revenge on Scopas and rewarding Simonides.

The most remarkable part of the story was that Simonides was able to identify the bodies, for their relatives, by remembering the sequence in which they had been sitting at the banquet table. This experience led Simonides to realize the principles of memory, of which he is supposedly the inventor. He had discovered that the fundamental key to a good memory is the ordered arrangement of the objects to be remembered.

According to Cicero:

'He inferred that persons desiring to train this faculty must select places and form mental images of the things they wish to remember and store those images in the places, so that the order of the places will preserve the order of the things, and the images of the things will denote the things themselves. We should then use the places and images respectively, as if they were a wax writing tablet, with the letters written on it.'

SOPHOCLES OUTWITS THE YOUNGER GENERATION

Sophocles (c. 496–405 BC) is best known as one of the great figures of Greek drama, writing over a hundred items, most of them satirical plays. His greatest masterpiece, though, is the tragedy *Oedipus Tyrannus*, on which Aristotle based his aesthetic theory of drama, and from which Freud derived the name and function of the 'Oedipus complex'. Sophocles was also an outstanding poet, winning first prize 18 times at the Great Dionysia – the most prestigious and important biennial poetry competition in Athens.

What is less well known about Sophocles is that he was also a giant polymath, specializing in a huge variety of fields. In addition to his literary achievements, he was a leading member of the Athens government, as well as being a senior general in the Athenian army. A contemporary parallel would be if Senator Bob Dole also combined the roles of General Colin Powell and playwright Arthur Miller.

Sophocles lived to a vast age. In his eighties he was charged by his son that his mental faculties had waned. His son further claimed that this rendered him incompetent to run his own affairs and that all matters should thus be passed on to him. Sophocles, however, was unwilling to accede. Naturally, he was a wealthy man and his son's demands would have resulted in a substantial transfer of riches, power and social influence. The situation could not be amicably resolved, so Sophocles' son took him to court, with the aim of publicly proving the decline in his father's mental abilities and thus wresting control of his affairs from him.

When the case opened, Sophocles conducted his own defence: 'Here is the script of a tragedy which I have just completed,' he informed the presiding judge. 'If you doubt my mental competence, take the script away and I will recite it in its entirety.' His request was granted and when Sophocles reached the second act, without having made a single mistake, the case against him was thrown out of court.

MEDIEVAL MEMORY THEATRES

A delightful book on the development of intelligence and memory is *The Day the Universe Changed* by James Burke. It is richly illustrated and gives a pleasant tour through an age that gave rise to the birth of intelligence. We shall now summarize a succinct and entertaining little essay taken from this book, on memory techniques in the Middle Ages, which are still totally valid today.

In a world where few were literate, good memory was essential. It was for this reason that rhyme, a useful *aide-mémoire*, was the prevalent form of literature at the time. Up to the fourteenth century almost everything, except legal documents, was written in rhyme. French merchants used a poem made up of 137 rhyming couplets, which contained all the rules of commercial arithmetic.

Given the cost of writing materials, a trained memory was a necessity for the scholar, as much as for the merchant. For more specific tasks than day to-day recall, medieval professionals used a learning aid that had originally been composed in classical times. The text they learnt from was called *Ad Herennium* (written from 86–82 BC by an anonymous teacher of rhetoric in Rome, and named after the dedicatee, one C. Herennius), and it was the major mnemonic reference work used in the Middle Ages.

It provided a technique for recalling vast quantities of material by means of the use of 'memory theatres'. The material to be memorized had to be conceived of as a familiar location. This could take the form of a building. If the building were too large, accuracy of recall would suffer. If it were too small, the separate parts of what was to be recalled would be too close to each other for individual recall. If it were too bright, it would blind the memory. Too dark, and it would obscure the material to be remembered.

Each separate part of the location was to be thought of as being about 3 ft (1 m) apart, so as to keep each major segment of the material isolated from the others. Once the memory theatre was prepared in this way, the process of memorizing would involve the memorizer in a mental walk through the building. The route had to be one that was logical and habitual, so that it might easily and naturally be recalled. The theatre was now ready to be fitted with the material to be memorized.

THE USE OF EXAGGERATION

This material took the form of mental images representing the different elements to be recalled. *Ad Herennium* advised that strong or highly exaggerated images were best, so reasons should be found to make the data stand out. The images should be funny, or gaudy, ornamented, unusual, outrageous, and so on. If trying to remember the Queen of Clubs in a card sequence, for instance, you could imagine Queen Elizabeth I swinging a golf club!

These images were to act as 'agents' of memory, and each image would trigger recall of several components of the material. If a legal argument were being memorized, for instance, then a dramatic scene might be appropriate. At the relevant point in the journey through the memory theatre this scene would be triggered and played out, reminding the memorizer of the points to be recalled.

The stored images could also relate to individual words, strings of words or entire arguments. Onomatopoeia, the use of words that sound like the action they describe, was particularly helpful in this regard.

The great medieval theologian St Thomas Aquinas particularly recommended the theatrical use of imagery for the recall of religious matters. 'All knowledge has its origins in sensation,' he said. The truth was accessible through visual aids.

As painting and sculpture began to appear in churches, the same techniques for recall were applied. Church imagery took on the form of memory agents. In Giotto's paintings of 1306 on the interior of the Arena Chapel in Padua, the entire series of images is structured as a memory theatre. Each Bible story illustrated is told through the medium of a figure or group in a separate place, made more memorable by the use of the recently developed artistic illusion of perspective. The chapel is a mnemonic path to salvation. Cathedrals became enormous memory theatres built to aid the worshippers to recall the details of Heaven and Hell.

The memory theatre is just as valid a technique now as it was in 80 BC, and we advise you to consider its use, in conjunction with Mind Mapping, to increase your own memory skills. Indeed, Mind Maps offer a particularly rich field for colourful and outrageous juxtapositions to assist your memory.

SIXTY YEARS OF CONDUCTING

One individual who used a similar system, and demonstrated its powers over the length of his career and into great age, was the Italian conductor Arturo Toscanini (1867–1957). He is widely regarded as the greatest ever orchestral conductor. For more than 60 years from the mid-1880s he conducted the world's leading orchestras in a uniquely individual and exciting fashion. His introduction to conducting was sensational: he had trained as a cellist and was touring with an opera company in Brazil in 1886 when he was asked, at the eleventh hour, to take over the baton, due to the unpopularity of the incompetent local conductor, against whom the Italian singers had gone on strike. However, the partisan audience had taken this as a national slur and had chased off the original Italian replacement. In a situation of complete uproar Toscanini was asked to step into the breach and overcome the hostility of the crowd, hardly the most auspicious circumstances for any performer. But his surprise début, at only 20 years of age, received rave reviews from the

highly critical Rio press and was noteworthy for another feat: Toscanini conducted the whole piece, Verdi's *Aïda*, without reference to the score, a practice
that he retained throughout his career. After this initial triumph Toscanini,
not surprisingly, conducted for the rest of the tour.

Later he was to admit to one short memory lapse on that first tense occasion, but this was very much an exception. The pianist and composer Ferruccio
Busoni reported in 1911:

> 'His memory is a phenomenon in the annals of physiology; but this does
> not impede his other faculties... He had just studied the very difficult
> score of Dukas's *Ariane et Barbe-bleue* and the next morning he was going
> to take the first rehearsal — from memory!'

PROVERBIAL MEMORY

Another witness to Toscanini's powers was the famous composer Igor
Stravinsky:

> 'Conducting an orchestra without the score has become the fashion, and
> is often a matter of mere display. There is, however, nothing marvellous
> about this apparent *tour de force*... one risks little and with a modicum of
> assurance and coolness a conductor can easily get away with it. It does not
> really prove that he knows the orchestration of the score. But there can
> be little doubt in the case of Toscanini. His memory is proverbial; there
> is not a detail that escapes him, as attendance at one of his rehearsals is
> enough to demonstrate.'

The impressions of these two important musical figures are reinforced by
many other stories of Toscanini's memory feats. There was the famous occasion, for example, when the NBC Symphony Orchestra had scheduled the
Prologue to Boito's *Mefistofele*, only to discover the night before rehearsal that
the scores for the backstage band had been mislaid. Toscanini simply sat down
and wrote them out from memory.

EYE SIGNALS

But why did Toscanini feel the need to conduct without a score in the first place? Undoubtedly, because he found it easy to do so, and perhaps also partly because of his short-sightedness, but more importantly because he realized that it enabled him to communicate much more effectively with the orchestra and to concentrate on the sound being made, instead of constantly having to refer to the score. Conductors communicate with musicians not only with their hands, but also with their eyes, and Toscanini wanted to use his eyes to signal key messages to the orchestra. Remember, eye-contact with the audience is also valuable when giving a presentation or lecture...

Toscanini did not just recall scores parrot-fashion; he also had a clear idea of the exact way the score should sound, and he would fine-tune this with rigorous study of even very familiar pieces before each new performance. His absolute dedication and unrivalled musicianship enabled him to conduct some of the greatest performances of the twentieth century, though he remained a modest man: 'I am no genius. I have created nothing. I play the music of other men. I am just a musician.'

Toscanini would not accept that in producing a perfect performance of a work he was in some way interpreting it:

'I have often heard people speaking of the *Eroica* of Conductor X, the *Siegfried* of Conductor Y, and the *Aïda* of Conductor Z. And I have always wondered what Beethoven, Wagner and Verdi would have said about the interpretation of these gentlemen, as if, through them, their works assumed a new paternity. I think that confronted by the *Eroica, Siegfried, Aïda,* an interpreter, entering as deeply as possible into the spirit of the composer, should only be willing to render the *Eroica* of Beethoven, the *Siegfried* of Wagner, and the *Aïda* of Verdi.'

Toscanini was also remarkably versatile: he did not just perform Beethoven, Wagner, Verdi and other established composers. During his early years as a conductor he gave world premières of such famous pieces as Leoncavallo's *I Pagliacci* and Puccini's *La Bohème* and later regularly performed the work of Strauss, Debussy and Sibelius.

MEMORY STORE

At the end of his career (he was still active at the age of 85) it is estimated that Toscanini had 250 symphonic works, 100 operas and numerous chamber pieces and songs stored in his memory. Late in life he was challenged to recall from memory some of his own youthful compositions, which he had written 60 or 70 years before and not looked at since. With only a few discrepancies he remembered them perfectly, text included. We shall see, shortly, how Toscanini's pupil, Sir Georg Solti, plans to crack his mentor's longevity performance record.

DOMINIC O'BRIEN

We have already encountered the three-times World Memory Champion in Chapter Six, where his exploits as winner of the Brain Trust's 'Brain of the Year' Award were briefly chronicled.

At an age (late thirties) when Academia tells us that creativity is a thing of the past, O'Brien decided to acquire and master a totally new mental skill and discipline – memory. Within seven years he had twice won the World Memory Championship, secured the laurels in the World Memory Matchplay Championship, written two books on memory and, as his most recent feat, has memorized 15 full packs of cards with no errors, under severe competition conditions, in just one hour!

This record was achieved during the Festival of the Mind at London's Royal Albert Hall on 21 April 1995.

'I PLAN TO HIT MY PEAK AT 95!'

O'Brien became interested in memory in early 1988, when he watched memory expert Creighton Carvello memorize a pack of cards on the television programme *Record Breakers*. Intrigued by this, he sat down with a pack of cards and set about devising his own memory system. His first attempt was far from auspicious – he took 26 minutes and made 11 errors. He persisted, however, and it was not long before he could memorize not just one pack of cards, but several. He achieved his first record of six packs at County Sound Radio, Guildford, in June 1988.

O'Brien was further motivated by the film *Rain Man*, in which Dustin Hoffman plays an autistic savant with a phenomenal memory. In one scene in the film, Hoffman uses his talent to help his brother (played by Tom Cruise) clean up at the blackjack tables in Las Vegas. This struck O'Brien as a potentially lucrative outlet for his own talent, and he spent the next six months analysing blackjack and developing his strategy for success. Unfortunately, his meal ticket proved to be a temporary one. Casinos are wise to the techniques of card memorizers and O'Brien is now banned from most of them.

In 1991 he participated in the first ever World Memory Championship, held at the Athenaeum Club in London. This was organized by the co-authors of this book. In the final, the competitors were lined up head-to-head, and each was given a pack of cards. On Dominic's left was the man who had inspired him to start on a career in memory, Creighton Carvello (whose professional background was in nursing). Dominic began to deal, turning the cards over faster and faster, until Creighton lost his concentration. O'Brien won the event and assumed the title of World Memory Champion.

O'Brien does not recognize any limits to the potential of human memory, and has continued to improve on his records and set ever more impressive ones. His achievements include: memorization of a pack of cards in 55 seconds; 35 packs of cards (this particular task took 13 hours) and the entire set of Trivial Pursuit questions.

The mathematical symbol Pi (the ratio of the circumference of a circle to its diameter) has exerted a fascination over mathematicians for millennia. Pi, which starts 3.14159265..., is a transcendental number, which means that it continues indefinitely, without ever dissolving into a repetitive sequence of digits. As such, it is an excellent tool for memory tests. O'Brien is currently planning an assault on the first 50,000 digits of Pi. This is a phenomenal

> ### BRAIN FLASH
>
> #### MEMORY TRAINING: A CURE FOR BLOCKED BRAINS
>
> *O'Brien's feats should serve as inspiration for anyone who wants to use his or her brain in a more efficient manner. After all, in an age of motorized transport, being able to run short distances very quickly is not a socially useful skill, but that does not prevent us from wanting to keep fit or from marvelling at the achievements of athletes such as Linford Christie and Sally Gunnell. Everyone who feels their brain may have become slightly flabby and who is daunted at the prospect of, for example, learning a new language should take inspiration from O'Brien's achievements. **Training your memory is a form of aerobics for the mind, which is especially valuable — indeed, vital — as you age.***

amount of information to store in the memory; just to read out 50,000 digits at the rate of one per second would take over 14 hours. Nevertheless, he is confident that he can commit the number to memory over a period of just two weeks.

WHAT SHOULD I DO NOW?

1. Absorb the message contained in the medieval memory theatre and classical memory techniques, such as the Roman room, as explained in this chapter.
2. Use the colourful, dramatic and visual impact of Mind Maps to help yourself remember key lists, ideas and facts.
3. Begin by making a conscious effort to remember the names of people you are introduced to at meetings or parties. Try to link their appearance with their name, or find out one singular and memorable fact about them that will aid your recall.
4. Move on to memorizing information in books, then progress to new mind sports, languages, and gradually become more ambitious!

CHAPTER TWELVE

THE LONG-LIVED PHOENIX

——

'IF I HAD MY LIFE TO LIVE OVER AGAIN, I WOULD HAVE MADE A RULE TO READ SOME POETRY AND LISTEN TO SOME MUSIC AT LEAST ONCE A WEEK FOR, PERHAPS, THE PARTS OF MY BRAIN NOW ATROPHIED WOULD THUS HAVE BEEN KEPT ACTIVE THROUGH USE.'

CHARLES DARWIN

INTRODUCTION

We have so far covered the theory, the physiology and the philosophy of improving with age, and have set you various challenges and provided you with stimulation to assist you as you progress through life. Now we turn to examples of those who are challenging themselves, with brief profiles of modern, living people who started out with no special advantages in life, but have found ways of giving themselves fresh challenges as they age. By doing this, they nurture extra synaptic connections (see Chapter Four) and keep themselves mentally alert.

In some instances these examples show people who have already achieved extraordinary heights in later life; in other instances they depict people who are taking the necessary preparatory steps in order to launch themselves into their golden age. In this chapter we deliberately avoid historical geniuses, intellectual superstars and so on, to demonstrate that anyone can substantially improve their prognosis, using the strategy we outline.

> **BRAIN FLASH**
>
> *A TEARAWAY AT 85*
> The Times of Saturday, 22 July 1995 *reported that 85-year-old Mr Arthur Wellstead is still tearing around on his 80 mph Yamaha 350cc bike.*
>
> *Meanwhile Edward Newsom has gone into the record books as Britain's oldest motorist at 104 years old, and still driving his G-registered 1.6L Ford Escort each morning to his office for a day's work.*

RENEGADES FROM THE NORM

If you think about it, all of us know people who contradict the normal negative stereotypes associated with ageing. These people, whom we describe here as **Renegades from the Norm,** are intelligent, active, ambitious, inquisitive, stimulating and generally fun to be with. The term is particularly appropriate, for it comes from the root word 'run-a-gate', meaning one who has escaped. In this instance, the individuals we are discussing have managed to escape from the downward curve of the mental aptitude norm.

In this chapter we not only profile notable examples of people who refuse to 'wind down', but also show the measures being taken by those in a younger age group to challenge themselves in true Goethean style, as an effective weapon against the encroaching years. Such measures include starting up entirely new careers well after the age of conventional retirement; acquiring awe-inspiring new mental skills; striving for extraordinary artistic goals; and, on a personal level, setting oneself extreme self-challenges of physical and mental endurance. The latter include plans, by a 40-plus UK business executive, to climb Mount Everest and walk to the North Pole.

One technique used by chess Grand Master Ray Keene (aged 47 at the time of writing this book) to stretch his mental capacities is regularly (at least twice a month) to take on up to 40 opponents at chess at one and the same time. His adversaries in such displays are not restricted to weak pushovers, but standardly include former British champions and players who have earned the title of International Master. **Ray Keene's best exploit so far (which he claims as a world percentage/speed record) was to win 101 games, draw 5 and lose 1 in just three hours.** After such displays he stretches himself even further by showing the moves of all the games, *from memory*, to the participants.

Staying with the mind sports analogy (which is, of course, just one of many possible strategies), Tony Buzan set himself the task, at the age of 53, of mastering the fiendishly difficult and complicated Japanese national board game 'Go'. Statisticians have calculated that 'Go' is infinitely more involved than even chess, in terms of the sheer number of possible moves that can be made.

Yet, in the space of a mere eight months at the start of 1995, Tony raised his skills in the game to near black-belt level, from where he could even seriously challenge Western champions and Japanese Dan players.

Now let us see how a variety of people, over a broad canvas, are challenging and re-inventing themselves like that mythical bird, the self-generating phoenix, as they age. Such people maintain, and even extend, their mental fitness, strength and alertness.

Profile of Frank Felberbaum (aged 58)

To launch this chapter, we spoke to one of the international brain stars of memory, Frank Felberbaum, of the Felberbaum Consulting Group Inc. Memory Training Systems. Here are his thoughts on the ageing brain, as it affects him and what he is doing, as part of an ongoing programme, to challenge himself:

1. 'As you age, you can *expand your brain,* just as you *expand a business.*
2. The ageing brain loves newness and the exotic. The Renegade from the Norm is the older person who can easily adapt to change, who likes learning new things and enjoys going to new places. Sometimes living with someone who has these characteristics can produce the same benefits.
3. Just as it used to be important to *have* the right connections to succeed in business and life, so now it is necessary to *make* the right connections in order to keep your ageing brain successful.
4. Memory is a conscious, pro-active creative process. If we control that process, we can control our memory and thus keep the ageing brain young and vital.
5. The mind has to be jolted by absurdity, even though it seeks the familiar. Change is difficult but highly necessary in order to survive and enjoy ageing.
6. If a young person makes an error in memory, it is usually attributed to information overload. If, however, an older person commits the memory failure, the reason given is usually ageing. In most situations the older individual

just needs a little more time to respond with the same accuracy as the younger individual.

'The above points focus on my impressions of why the brain gets better as it gets older. The following is what I know about my own improving brain and memory.

'Since I am constantly training thousands of executives, managers, sales reps and technical staff in hundreds of corporations, I am constantly and consciously aware of my brain and memory and how and why it functions as it does.

'I am aware of the methods and techniques that I use and of the effort I expend to achieve my memory success and that of my many memory-workshop participants. This has kept my mind razor-sharp! I have been a professional in the corporate memory development arena for over 28

BRAIN FLASH

GREAT-GREAT-GRANDMA SWIMS TO WORLD RECORD

'Mary Maina plunged into the Chandler pool in Brisbane, and with spectators on their feet applauding her all the way, she set a world record for 50 metres freestyle — in 5 min 12.34 seconds. Two weeks ago, "Marvellous Mary", as she is known to friends, celebrated her 101st birthday.

Her swim, using sidestroke, stands as the fastest for the 100–104 age group, in which Maina was the only competitor at the World Masters Games. "I think I'm glad it's over. I was determined I would get to the end," said Maina, one of more than 23,000 competitors from 71 countries. Maina puts herself on a par with Kieren Perkins, Australia's magnificent long-distance swimmer, as the fastest in her particular branch of the sport. No matter that Perkins, who has set the world standard for 400, 800 and 1,500m, would have passed the 500-metre mark by the time the golden oldie had finished her 50.

Queenslander Maina, who has 12 great-great-grandchildren, began swimming as recreation when she was 60 and resisted the lure of competitive sport for 30 years before taking the plunge.

The oldest woman in Australia to have a heart pacemaker fitted, she brought with her a letter from her doctor, detailing her regular medication, just in case she was one of those selected for a drug test.'

years and have never reached a plateau. **I have trained my brain and memory to seek challenges and continuously learn new and stimulating ideas, concepts and skills. My prime objective for my clients and myself is to prevent business information loss,** hence the name of my training programme, the Business of Memory. What we learn takes a lifetime to acquire and an equal amount of energy, and it is too valuable to allow it to become part of the great disappearing act. Because of my unquenchable thirst for new knowledge about the brain and memory, it is digesting anything in its path. I can't wait to arise each morning to think, to learn and to teach.'

PROFILE OF THE TOVEYS

As an example of what can realistically be achieved by those who, judged by the customary standards of today, are 'over the hill', consider the cases of Brian and Mary Tovey (Sir Brian and Lady Tovey, to give them their correct formal designations).

NEW CAREER – AGED 57

Brian Tovey spent 33 years as a civil servant, ending with five years as director of GCHQ (the Government Communications Headquarters, or 'Cheltenham Spy Centre' beloved of the popular Press). Then, at the age of 57, he joined the Plessey Company, a career change that involved not only the wholesale acquisition of new and unfamiliar facts but the development of entirely novel and challenging skills. ('Before I joined Plessey,' he says, 'I could not even read a balance sheet. Plessey not only taught me to do this, but a whole range of essential business concepts.')

STARTING AFRESH YET AGAIN

At 62, he left Plessey and, ably aided and encouraged by his wife (of whom more anon), set up a consultancy, Cresswell Associates Ltd, whose avowed mission was (and is) to advise companies on their relations with the bureaucracies of Whitehall and Brussels. **Once again, new ideas, new knowledge and new attitudes had to be cultivated… at an age when not a few of his contemporaries were urging Brian to 'hang up his boots' (advice that he describes as a prescription for constructing his own coffin).** And Cresswell Associates has gone from strength to strength; turnover and profitability have grown year-on-year (recession notwithstanding), and the client list now includes two major multi-nationals, as well as a number of smaller companies. Sir Brian, who is now aged 70, is Chairman not only of his own company but of two others, Deputy Chairman of another and (an honorary title) Vice-President of the Federation of the Electronics Industry. So much for being 'over the hill'.

BRAIN FLASH

AGE-OLD WISDOM ON THE BENCH

'*Frederick Lawton says it would be wrong to ban judges over 65. The older the judge, the better he is likely to be.*

There is a saying among judges that during his first five years of appointment, the newcomer to the Bench should remember that he knows little about his job and that during the next five years he thinks he knows a lot but doesn't. It is only after ten years that he can consider himself reasonably competent. A judge appointed in his early fifties, as most judges are, would not be on top of his work until he was over 60 and in sight of retirement at 65.

The conscientious judge — and most are — is aware that he learns more about his job every day he sits. He never stops learning. Time and time again he says to himself, after making a decision with which he is not entirely satisfied, "I'll never do that again." As the years go by, the memory acquires a larger and larger store of judicial "don'ts". Providing a judge has good health, particularly good mental health, he is likely to become a better judge as he gets older. The two best judges in my professional lifetime, Lord Reid and Lord Denning, both delivered some of their best judgements when well into their seventies. What a loss to jurisprudence there would have been, had they been obliged to retire at 65.

As Lord Justice of Appeal, I had the privilege of sitting with Lord Denning. I was 60 when I went to the Court of Appeal. I had been a High Court judge for 11 years. Lord Denning was about 68. Every time I sat with him I learnt more about judging.'

Sir Frederick Lawton was a Lord Justice of Appeal, 1972–86.

'TIME-BETTERING DAYS' (SHAKESPEARE, SONNET 82)

Lady Tovey has arrived at a similar point by a different route. Starting life with an education that could be described as 'not better than just about adequate', she plunged with verve and determination into the world of commerce and industry – with a few years working for the British Embassy in Washington for good measure.

A year before their marriage, she joined Brian in setting up Cresswell Associates, of which she has now become Managing Director, with responsibility for developing a subset of the company that provides personal development training (Mind Mapping, memory systems, speed/range-reading, etc.), as well as for the financial and administrative aspects of the company as a whole.

As if that were not enough, she is also administrator of the Brain Trust, which, as we have seen, is a charity that funds those who want to develop their mental capabilities but lack the wherewithal to do so. In this capacity, she has played a key role in organizing major elements of its fund-raising, including the 'Festival of the Mind' at London's Royal Albert Hall in April 1995. All this at… well, ladies do not normally declare their age, and Mary has the looks and demeanour of a woman of 30, but in fact she recently celebrated her half-century, a fact that becomes believable only when you realize the depth, maturity and wisdom of her very considerable mind. A true renegade from the norm.

TIME'S BEST JEWEL

It only remains to add that Mary and Brian have a wide range of cultural interests, including music, art, ballet and opera, and that they enjoy a marriage that goes above and beyond mere happiness: the transcendent joy of their relationship with one another is something that all who know them recognize and treasure.

Such stable and contented relationships are absolutely central to maintaining your mental edge and balance as you age, as we have already seen from the life-expectancy chart in Chapter Two.

BRAIN FLASH

Age-old barriers no obstacle to Podkopayeva

'Were the researchers in the United States wasting their time? Between 1990 and 1993, three separate studies into the effects of ageing on athletes concluded that physiological decline begins well into the forties, not at 35, as scientists had thought. Then along came Yekaterina Podkopayeva, whose successes at 42 provided evidence worth a thousand studies.

Podkopayeva was the world's No.1-ranked woman 1,500-metre runner of 1994 and one of only two to break four minutes. In head-to-heads over the season, she ended 3–2 up on Sonia O'Sullivan, 25, the Irish world silver-medal winner, and 2–1 up on Hassiba Boulmerka, 26, the Algerian champion.

Now the commercial world has realized its mistake. A kit sponsor, who thought that a 40-something was not worth a contract, has signed her up.

According to Dr Owen Anderson, an American physiologist who publishes Running Research News, *loss of determination has a greater influence on declining performance than age itself.*

"We used to think that, at 35 or so, athletes began a steady physiological decline, but now we are finding out that most of what we thought was an age-related decline is due to reduction in training," Anderson said. "We are finding that runners who are able to continue their training with intense workouts do not lose much between 25 and 45.

"At 45, your race times may be slower, but it is not the ageing process that has given you leaden legs. It is probably reduced motivation, a reduction in quality training, and lack of consistency of training."'

PROFILE OF PROFESSOR BENJAMIN ZANDER (AGED 56)

A new force has entered the brain-research arena, namely, the force of music.

Benjamin Zander is the founder and conductor of the Boston Philharmonic Orchestra. He has led Boston's Youth Philharmonic Orchestra for 22 years and has taken them on 10 international concert tours. He teaches at the New England Conservatory and is Artistic Director of the music programme at Walnut Hill School for gifted children. His CD recordings of Beethoven's Ninth, Stravinsky's *Rite of Spring* and Mahler's Sixth Symphony with the Boston Philharmonic have gained international acclaim.

In early 1995 Professor Zander took an important step on his greatest challenge, which some cynics might have described instead as his most fool-hardy risk. He accepted an invitation to conduct one of Gustav Mahler's richest, deepest and most complex symphonies – the Sixth. What is strange about that, one might ask? After all, he is a conductor.

But this was the opening shot in Professor Zander's wider ambition to 'musicate the world'. And the difference was that Mahler's Sixth Symphony was to be performed at London's mighty Barbican Centre in front of an audience of thousands, with one of London's top professional orchestras, but with only a couple of days for them to rehearse in advance with a conductor they had never even seen before – let alone worked with – in their lives. What is more, Professor Zander had never before conducted in the British capital. This is the sort of challenge that most 50-plus-year-olds would gladly side-step. However, Zander's ambition to succeed remained indomitable. And this was the reaction of the critics.

The Sunday Times called Zander's 1995 London début concert, performing Mahler's Sixth Symphony with the London Philharmonic Orchestra 'spectacular' and 'memorable'. And famed author Gail Sheehy wrote:

> 'Ben Zander is that rare musician who can paint with words what he plays with music. For those of us who are not musicians he can conjure up the spirits and pulses of life and put us under music's spell.'

As a particularly interesting addendum, it has recently been discovered that music has a profound effect on the maturing brain.

THE EFFECT OF MUSIC ON IQ

Many scientists now believe that listening to certain types of music can make people more intelligent.

> **BRAIN FLASH**
>
> *TRUE WORKS OF GENIUS*
> '*I hold that of all Verdi's operas, only* Otello *and* Falstaff *are truly works of genius.*'
> *Bernard Levin*
>
> Verdi wrote Otello *in 1887, at the age of 74, and* Falstaff *in 1893, at the age of 80. They were the last two of his numerous operas.*

University of California physicist Dr Gordon Shaw examined brain responses during abstract reasoning tasks and found a pattern of activity resembling that of music. Together with psychologist Frances Rauscher (an ex-professional cellist), he then attempted to establish whether providing music training to young children could improve their spatial reasoning skills. The initial results were extremely positive: after three, six and nine months of lessons the children's abstract reasoning showed great improvement, just as predicted, and the fact that this was the only aspect that showed such improvement suggests that music was not simply attracting their attention, but training their brains.

IMPROVED IQ FOR THE OLDER AGE GROUP

Encouraged by these results, Shaw and Rauscher then decided to analyse what happens to adults when they listen to music. They compared three listening states: a Mozart piano sonata, a relaxation tape and silence, and tested spatial reasoning after each. Their results revealed that Mozart had an extremely positive effect.

What about other forms of music? Can listening to heavy rock, acid house or rap music have the same stimulating effect as Mozart? Shaw and Rauscher believe not, since these forms of music do not have the required structural and harmonic complexity. Shaw claims that:

'We are born with some of the structure, there are certain natural patterns that can be excited, and when we hear Mozart's music it is pleasing for us, because these natural patterns are being excited in our brain while we listen.'

MUSIC AND CHESS

It is also interesting to note, for those who are determined to improve their mental performance as they age and who are looking for a suitable activity to

---

BRAIN FLASH

ROLE MODEL

'Toscanini's pupil, the conductor Sir Georg Solti, now 82 and at the peak of his career, is one of the driving forces behind the Verdi Festival, organized by the Royal Opera House, London. This is planned to run from 1995 until 2001, with 4 Verdi operas being performed each year. In an interview on 10 June 1995, on the eve of his stupendous performance of La Traviata, Sir Georg announced that his ambition is to become the world's first active conductor at the age of 100.

La Traviata was performed during a heatwave which had London sweltering, and Sir Georg's sole concession to the freak temperatures was to remove his jacket whilst conducting: "the first time I ever did this in my life".'

---

help achieve this, that the experiments of Shaw and Rauscher indicated that a similar pattern of brainwave was occurring while listening to Mozart and while playing chess.

PROFILE OF RIKKI HUNT (AGED 42)

Rikki Hunt, Mind Mapper and Managing Director of a hugely successful company, is known as the originator of the concept of 'The Thinking Organization'. He challenges himself to achieve his potential by climbing

---

BRAIN FLASH

DON'T SAY 'CAN'T'

'Rikki Hunt is terrified of heights. But the summer of 1995 saw him scaling the lofty peaks of the Eiger and the Matterhorn. Why? To prove to his staff that anyone can do anything, given time and dedication.

Three juggling balls are displayed in Hunt's office in Swindon. Hunt cannot juggle but they are there to remind him he can learn to do so if he chooses.

"I believe very strongly that people can do anything they want," he says. "After years of being kicked down I have a life quest to teach people to realize their potential. There is no limit, and that is why our company slogan is: Don't say can't.""

---

mountains, such as the Eiger and the Matterhorn, and by walking to the North Pole. He now has Mount Everest in his sights.

Ask yourself which other group of human beings the Renegades in this chapter most closely resemble. The answer? Children!

And what do all the poets, philosophers, religious leaders and thinkers, in their various ways, say must be the impetus for the ageing human? 'You shall not enter the kingdom of heaven unless you become as a little child again.'

Or, as William Blake would have put it, 'You must leave the age of innocence (childhood), enter the age of experience (early middle age) and re-enter the age of innocence (advanced childhood), if you are to enter paradise.'

WHAT SHOULD I DO NOW?

1. Start listening to classical music to harmonize the full flow of your intelligence. Mozart, Haydn, Bach, Beethoven, Mahler and Stravinsky are particularly recommended.

2. Dream up an ambitious but realistic new challenge for yourself – and achieve it. It could be professional, cultural, sporting or in your hobby sphere.

3. Rely on yourself. Don't wait for others to help you or do it for you.

4. Remember Goethe's message from Chapter Five: 'In the beginning was the deed... Begin it now.'

BRAIN FLASH

OLDEST WORKING WOMAN
Hilda Ford is 93 and can claim to be the oldest working woman in the country. Her achievement was recognized in 1995 with the MBE. Her perhaps unlikely job is selling car accessories in Todmorden in Yorkshire, and even this does not absorb all her energies, for in her spare time she is a regular member of the local choral society.

CHAPTER THIRTEEN

HOW FIT IS YOUR BRAIN?

———

'WHAT CAN THE AVERAGE PERSON DO TO STRENGTHEN HIS OR HER MIND? THE IMPORTANT THING IS TO BE ACTIVELY INVOLVED IN AREAS UNFAMILIAR TO YOU.'

ARNOLD SCHEIBEL, HEAD OF BRAIN RESEARCH INSTITUTE, UCLA

INTRODUCTION

We have now seen a group of people, Renegades from the Norm, challenging themselves, extending their mental vistas. In this chapter we provide a smorgasbord of mental tests, mental self-checks, mental fitness gauges and the opening-up of new parameters, to find out just how fit your brain really is.

We explain how mind sports and brain callisthenics can become a way of keeping your brain fit as you age. We quote authoritative and fascinating research from the University of California at Irvine, which indicates that mind sports may help defend you against Alzheimer's Disease by building new brain circuitry.

As you age, is your brain fit? Is there room for improvement and, if so, how much? Later in this chapter you can test yourself in the areas of self- and time-management, the physical brain, emotional stability, sensual awareness, memory and creativity – and find out!

BRAIN FLASH

SEIZE YOUR OPPORTUNITIES

'Running a big business is like playing a game of chess: it requires vast logical analysis, and the courage to seize opportunities.'

THE BENEFITS OF MIND SPORTS AND PHYSICAL SPORTS

'Chess is the Gymnasium of the mind.'   V. I. LENIN

'I strongly approve of rational games, for they serve to perfect the art of thinking.'   GOTTFRIED LEIBNIZ

'Guru Hargobind (fl. 16th c.), Sixth Guru of the Sikhs, encouraged his followers to look to physical fitness, to learn martial arts and to become expert horsemen to protect the rights of themselves and others. Sikhs were to be "Sant Sipa" – Saint Soldiers.'   *The Times*, July 1994

CHESS – KING OF WESTERN MIND SPORTS

Why are mind games, and chess in particular, regarded as relevant and important? The answer is that, throughout the history of culture, prowess at mind games has been associated with intelligence in general. Mind sports do, indeed, play a vital part in the lives of many geniuses, and of the various occidental mind sports, chess is undoubtedly king. It is the one practised most

---

BRAIN FLASH

IT'S NEVER TOO LATE

'What can the average person do to strengthen his or her mind? The important thing is to be actively involved in areas unfamiliar to you. Anything that's intellectually challenging can probably serve as a kind of stimulus for dendritic growth, which means it adds to the computation reserves in your brain. **Do puzzles; try a musical instrument; repair something; try the arts; dance; date provocative people; try tournament bridge, chess;** *even sailboat racing. And remember, researchers agree that it's never too late. All of life should be a learning experience, because we are challenging our brain and therefore building brain circuitry. Literally, this is the way the brain operates.'*

Arnold Scheibel, head of the Brain Research Institute, UCLA, Los Angeles

---

widely and has the most well-doc-umented theory to back it up. A number of geniuses have rated chess highly. Goethe called the game 'the touchstone of the intellect'. Haroun Al-Rashid, the Abbasyd Caliph of Islam (AD 786–809) and the man idealized in the *Arabian Nights,* was the first of his dynasty to play chess.

The eleventh-century Byzantine Emperor, Alexius Comnenus, was allegedly playing chess when he was surprised by a murderous con-spiracy which, being a good chess player, he naturally managed to escape!

The Aladdin of the fairy tale was, in real life, a chess player, a lawyer from Samarkand in the court of Tamerlaine. Tamerlaine himself, the conqueror of half the known world during the fourteenth century, loved to play chess and named his son Shah Rukh, since Tamerlaine was moving a rook at the time the birth was announced. Another genius, Benjamin Franklin, was an enthusiastic chess player. Indeed, the first chess publication in America was Franklin's *Morals of Chess,* which appeared in 1786. Chess was mentioned by Shakespeare, Goethe, Leibniz and Einstein; Tsar Ivan the Terrible, Queen Elizabeth I, Catherine the Great and Napoleon all prided themselves on their chess skills.

Here and now we show you how to develop your own mental qualities, fol-lowing the example of chess and other mind sports champions.

BRAIN FLASH

THE FIRST 'OFFICIAL' MIND SPORT
One of the best ways to challenge your mind through chess is to tackle Ray Keene's daily winning move puzzle in The Times. *Here is one example, from the 'Immortal Game', played at Simpsons-in-the-Strand, London, 1851.*
QUESTION: White to play and force checkmate.
ANSWER: 1. Qf6 check Nxf6. 2. Be7. Checkmate.

THE GROWTH OF MIND SPORTS

Since the dawn of civilization some ten thousand years ago, history has recorded that human beings have been games players. The earliest writings of ancient civilizations regularly make reference to games similar in concept to tic-tac-toe (noughts and crosses). **As a civilization progressed, so did the complexity of its games.**

The development of games over the centuries has been a fascinating one, and has now reached a point that will inevitably lead to an evolutionary change in the way in which we engage in combat, entertain ourselves and think about our intelligence.

INTERNATIONAL BRAIN STARS

A measure of the growth of interest in mind sports is reflected in the increased prize fund for major contests. In 1969 the World Chess Championship match was worth around 3,000 roubles (less than $3,000) to the winner. In 1990 Kasparov and Karpov contested a purse of $2 million. Just three years later, that price practically doubled again for the Kasparov–Short match, with the total investment in the match now approaching $10 million.

Concurrent with the explosion of interest in chess and mind sports has come a similar explosion of interest in measuring general mental skills, competing in them and forming organizations based on them. Witness the dramatic growth of Mensa, whose membership in England alone increases by over 2,000 per year, that membership having as one of its major hobbies the playing of chess, other mind sports and the solving of mental puzzles. Similarly, we have seen the recent formation of the International Brain Club (for information on how to join, see page 175), with its emphasis on teaching mental skills, its formation of the Chess League for Schools and its establishment of official mental world records in each of the areas of mind sports and mental literacy.

The mental world records are identical in form to the physical world records. They include the memorization of the symbol Pi, the fastest speed for the memorization of cards or numbers, the highest IQs, top chess ratings and other mental feats that were accomplished either by isolated individuals or in mental competitions. The Brain Trust Charity, in conjunction with the International Brain Clubs and their panel of experts, gives official authorization/recognition to such records.

This growth of interest in the mental arena has become all-pervasive. Local, national and international competitions proliferate: virtually all major newspapers and magazines carry articles, columns and feature sections on chess, bridge and brain-twisters. In recent years the 'Tournament of the Mind' in *The Times* and the *Mastermind* programme on BBC television have attracted large followings. Hundreds of competitors descend on towns and cities for chess, bridge, 'Go', 'Scrabble', 'Monopoly' and other championships, and the demand for literature, clubs, playing venues and competitions steadily increases.

Evidence is growing that the dominance of physical sports, as the more popular medium of human expression over mental sports, is not the reflection of an innate preference but simply the reflection of a lack of opportunity to express what is an equal, if not greater, interest in the mental arena. For with the growth of information technology and electronic data systems we have reached a point in history where, for the first time, competition on the mental battlefield can be seen, instantaneously, by as many spectators as watch competitions on the physical battlefield. World Chess Championship matches are being transmitted to billions of viewers worldwide, through television, faxes, Teletext and the Internet. The global interest in mental world championship contests can thus be seen as the result of a natural interest by the human mind in its own function and in the way in which it can develop games to test its limits. The phenomenon is common to all games, as the statistics on those interested in the different mental arenas more than adequately prove.

PUMPING UP YOUR BRAIN POWER

A new study, reported in the journal *Nature*, shows that both physical and mental exercise can keep the brain sharp into old age and might help prevent

Alzheimer's Disease and other mental disorders that accompany ageing. The study, by Dr Carl Cotman of the University of California at Irvine, is the first to show a direct link between physical and mental activity, and demonstrates that growth factors in the brain can be controlled by exercise. There is already a great deal of evidence to suggest that those who exercise regularly live longer and score higher marks in mental tests. Cotman's findings add important weight to the necessity for physical activity to combat the ageing process. According to Cotman: **'The brain really is a muscle. When you exercise it, the mind grows and is capable of handling more projects and complex problems.'**

Cotman used rodents in his research, as rats have similar exercise habits to humans, with similar effects. The rats were allowed to choose how much exercise they wanted to do and each demonstrated individual characteristics. Some were lazy 'couch' rats, rarely getting on the treadmill, while others were 'runaholics', obsessively running for hours every night. Those that exercised, however, showed much higher levels of BDNF (brain-derived neurotrophic factor), an important growth factor in the brain.

It appears that there is an ideal threshold of exercise that provides the maximum possible benefit, and Cotman's results demonstrated that those rats that exercised excessively showed no better growth than those that exercised around the optimum level.

SLIMMING TO SUCCESS

Meanwhile, a new Canadian study, focusing on the severely obese, has found that obesity can cause sleep disturbances, which may lead to learning disorders and a significant drop in IQ. Dr Susan Rhodes, a psychologist at the Medical University of South Carolina in Charleston, claims that obesity causes a decrease of oxygen in the brain during sleep, due to fat in the throat or to a more indirect means involving the central nervous system, leading to a type of brain damage. She also suggests that putting the obese on diets may reverse the damage and 'make them smarter'.

> ### BRAIN FLASH
>
> *RESEARCH SHOWS THE MIND IS CAPABLE OF GROWTH IN OLD AGE*
> *'Researchers can now demonstrate that certain crucial areas of human intelligence do not decline in old age among people who are generally healthy.*
>
> *The new research challenges beliefs long held both by scientists and the public and suggests that, among people who remain physically and emotionally healthy, some of the most important forms of intellectual growth can continue well into the eighties. It also suggests that decline in intelligence can be reversed in some instances and that earlier notions about the loss of brain cells, as a person ages, were in error.*
>
> *Countless intellectually vigorous lives may have atrophied on the mistaken assumption that old age brings an unavoidable mental deterioration.*
>
> *"The expectation of a decline is a self-fulfilling prophecy," said Werner Schaie, a researcher on ageing. "Those who don't accept the stereotype of a helpless old age, but instead feel they can do as well in old age as they have at other times in their lives, don't become ineffective before their time."'*

Finally, remember: if you are trying to develop a challenging new mental skill, such as Mind Mapping, chess or 'Go', are trying to improve your diet, or give up smoking, then refer back to our vitally important section in Chapter Four on transforming a Big Bad Habit into a Good New Habit. Meta-positive thinking is the way to change yourself for the better and you cannot start soon enough. This is a key component of the strategy for successful ageing.

HOW FIT IS YOUR BRAIN?

What sort of shape is your brain in? The following questionnaire tests you in important areas of your brain power. Identify your strengths – and the areas that need improvement.

Circle a number for each answer, and then note your total score for each section.

SELF- AND TIME-MANAGEMENT	YES	NOT SURE/ SOMETIMES	NO
1. DO YOU HAVE A CLEAR VISION OF WHAT YOU WANT FROM LIFE?	(2)	(1)	(0)
2. DO YOU CARRY MORE THAN 50 PAGES OF 'DIARY MATERIAL'?	(0)	(1)	(2)
3. ARE YOU PUNCTUAL?	(2)	(1)	(0)
4. DO YOU USE IMAGES, SYMBOLS AND COLOURS IN YOUR DIARY?	(2)	(1)	(0)
5. DO YOU REGULARLY FEEL STRESSED?	(0)	(1)	(2)
6. DO YOU LIKE PLANNING?	(2)	(1)	(0)
7. DO YOU PLAN REGULAR HOLIDAYS AND BREAKS FOR YOURSELF?	(2)	(1)	(0)
8. DO YOU FEEL GUILTY IF YOU'RE NOT WORKING?	(0)	(1)	(2)
9. DO YOU REMEMBER YOUR LIFE IN INDIVIDUAL YEARS?	(2)	(1)	(0)
10. DO YOU REGULARLY REVIEW YOUR LIFE?	(2)	(1)	(0)
11. DO YOU GENERALLY LOOK FORWARD TO TOMORROW?	(2)	(1)	(0)
12. DO YOU FEEL THREATENED BY YOUR DIARY?	(0)	(1)	(2)

THE PHYSICAL BRAIN	YES	NOT SURE/ SOMETIMES	NO
1. DO YOU EAT (AND LIKE!) LOTS OF SUGAR AND/OR SALT?	(0)	(1)	(2)
2. DO YOU REGULARLY EAT FRESH VEGETABLES AND FRUIT?	(2)	(1)	(0)
3. DO YOU EAT A LOT OF REFINED FOODS?	(0)	(1)	(2)
4. ARE YOU CONSIDERABLY OVER- OR UNDER-WEIGHT?	(0)	(1)	(2)
5. DO YOU TAKE (AND ENJOY) REGULAR EXERCISE?	(2)	(1)	(0)
6. DO YOU HAVE REGULAR HEALTH CHECKS?	(2)	(1)	(0)
7. DO YOU DRINK EXCESSIVELY?	(0)	(1)	(2)
8. DO YOU REGULARLY TAKE DRUGS OF ANY SORT?	(0)	(1)	(2)
9. DO YOU GRILL RATHER THAN FRY FOODS?	(2)	(1)	(0)
10. DO YOU HAVE A VARIED DIET?	(2)	(1)	(0)

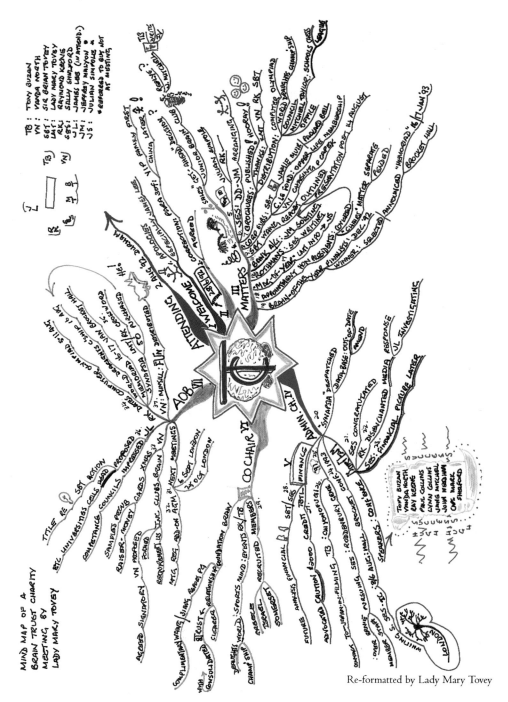

Re-formatted by Lady Mary Tovey

ABOVE: Lady Tovey's Mind Map of a charity meeting shows how a mass of information can be encapsulated in a very compact space.

The Austrian National Library

ABOVE: Tests have shown that listening to Mozart's music can have a positive effect on IQ and abstract reasoning skills.

BELOW: Co-author Ray Keene (back to camera) takes on multiple opponents in a simultaneous chess display.

THE PHYSICAL BRAIN (CONTINUED)	YES	NOT SURE/ SOMETIMES	NO
11. DO YOU DRINK MORE THAN SIX CUPS OF TEA AND/OR COFFEE PER DAY?	(0)	(1)	(2)
12. ARE YOU A SMOKER?	(0)	(1)	(2)

EMOTIONAL STABILITY	YES	NOT SURE/ SOMETIMES	NO
1. ARE YOU SELF-CONFIDENT?	(2)	(1)	(0)
2. ARE YOU ABLE TO CRY?	(2)	(1)	(0)
3. DO YOU OFTEN GET ANNOYED?	(0)	(1)	(2)
4. DO PEOPLE GENERALLY CONSIDER YOU A HAPPY PERSON?	(2)	(1)	(0)
5. DO YOU MAINTAIN FRIENDSHIPS OVER A LONG PERIOD OF TIME?	(2)	(1)	(0)
6. DO YOU OFTEN FEEL HELPLESS?	(0)	(1)	(2)
7. IS LIFE OFTEN A BURDEN?	(0)	(1)	(2)
8. DO YOU GET ALONG WITH YOUR FAMILY?	(2)	(1)	(0)
9. DO YOU SAY WHAT YOU FEEL?	(2)	(1)	(0)
10. DO YOU LIKE TO TOUCH AND BE TOUCHED?	(2)	(1)	(0)
11. DO YOU FEEL HAPPY WHEN OTHERS FEEL HAPPY?	(2)	(1)	(0)
12. DO YOU GENERALLY KEEP YOUR FEARS TO YOURSELF?	(0)	(1)	(2)

SENSUAL AWARENESS	YES	NOT SURE/ SOMETIMES	NO
1. DO YOU ENJOY DANCING?	(2)	(1)	(0)
2. DO YOU REGULARLY ENJOY FILMS, PLAYS, PAINTINGS AND MUSIC?	(2)	(1)	(0)
3. ARE YOU ABLE TO RECALL VISUAL INFORMATION CLEARLY?	(2)	(1)	(0)

SENSUAL AWARENESS (CONTINUED)	YES	NOT SURE/ SOMETIMES	NO
4. ARE YOU ABLE TO RECALL SMELLS AND TASTES CLEARLY?	(2)	(1)	(0)
5. DO YOU RECALL SOUNDS, TACTILE SENSATIONS AND PHYSICAL MOVEMENTS CLEARLY?	(2)	(1)	(0)
6. DO YOU EAT TO LIVE, NOT LIVE TO EAT?	(0)	(1)	(2)
7. ARE YOU SENSUAL?	(2)	(1)	(0)
8. DO YOU ENJOY PLAYING WITH CHILDREN?	(2)	(1)	(0)
9. DO YOU LIKE YOUR BODY?	(2)	(1)	(0)
10. DO YOU LIKE NATURE?	(2)	(1)	(0)
11. DO OTHERS CONSIDER YOU WELL-DRESSED?	(2)	(1)	(0)
12. DO YOU DISLIKE DRIVING?	(0)	(1)	(2)

MEMORY TEST 1
LONG-TERM MEMORY

On a piece of paper, write down the names of the planets of the solar system, in order of distance from the sun.

MEMORY TEST 2
RECALL DURING LEARNING

Read through the following list of words once, and then carry out the instruction that follows:

1. Cage	9. of	17. the	25. will
2. exact	10. the	18. wood	26. afraid
3. his	11. the	19. door	27. join
4. pan	12. of	20. glass	28. ceiling
5. foot	13. wide	21. of	29. top
6. page	14. Leonardo da Vinci	22. of	30. finger
7. high	15. Rainy	23. turn	31. fire
8. and	16. tiny	24. up	

Without looking at the words again, write down as many as you can remember on a piece of paper, and then refer to the scoring.

CREATIVITY

Before proceeding, make sure that you have a pen and pencil, and a watch so that you can time yourself for a minute. Then do the following:

Write down, in one minute, as fast as you can, all the uses you can possibly think of for an elastic band.

HOW FIT IS YOUR BRAIN? ANSWERS

SELF- AND TIME-MANAGEMENT

SCORING:

18–24 Excellent. You are working at something like maximum efficiency.

12–17 Good, but there is plenty of room for improvement.

6–11 Could (and should) try harder.

0–5 You are not using anything like the full power of your brain and body.

THE PHYSICAL BRAIN

SCORING:

18–24 Excellent. You are giving your brain every opportunity to flourish.

12–17 Good, but you may not be looking after yourself quite as well as you think.

6–11 You may be losing out mentally by underestimating the importance of physical health to a sharp mind.

0–5 You are undermining your brain power by bodily abuse. Give your brain a chance.

EMOTIONAL STABILITY

SCORING:

18–24 You are unusually mature emotionally.

12–17 You are generally mature but would benefit from working on this area.

6–11 You undervalue yourself – wrongly.

0–5 Pay attention to this aspect of your mind.

SENSUAL AWARENESS

SCORING:

18–24 Excellent. You live a well-balanced, sensual, cultural and physical life, and your brain benefits as a result.

12–17 A good score, on which you would do well to build.

6–11 An average score, but not a particularly good one. Remember that there is more to thinking than dry theorizing.

0–5 You are in danger of starving your brain of stimulation. Enjoy yourself!

MEMORY TEST 1

ANSWER: Mercury, Venus, Earth, Mars, Jupiter, Saturn, Uranus, Neptune, Pluto. Score one point for each planet that you placed correctly.

SCORING:

8–9 Exceptional

6–7 Very good and well above average

4–5 Still above average

2–3 Average to just above average

1–2 Surprisingly, quite normal

The reason for the generally low score on a subject such as this, to which our brains have been exposed in both school and general life, is that we have not been trained to use our long-term memories.

MEMORY TEST 2

SCORING:

You will probably find that you recalled at least one of the words that were repeated (of, the), that you remembered Leonardo da Vinci (because it 'stood out') and that, of all the other words, you remembered more from the begin-ning and end, plus words from the middle that were in some way associated with each other or meant something special to you. If you remembered all the words, you have a quite exceptionally well-trained memory. If not, don't worry. But if you think that remembering such a list is completely beyond your capabilities, you are wrong. Study the methods in this book and you will find that you can.

CREATIVITY

SCORING:

The normal score on this creativity test, based on the work of E. Paul Torrence, ranges from 0 to an average of 3–4, an excellent of 8, a very unusual score of 12, and an exceptional score of 16.

CONCLUSION

Our brain-fitness questionnaire may have revealed to you areas of your life that you feel you want to change or improve. These might, for example, include the following: becoming more decisive; adopting a more healthy diet; starting aerobic exercise; or improving your memory and creativity skills – all of these within the context of designing successful ageing strat-egies for yourself.

If you do want to change any aspect of your life, as a result of having completed this quiz, now is the time to review our comments on trans-forming a Big Bad Habit into a Good New Habit (see Chapter Four). Remember the power of meta-positive thinking – 'the power to change yourself for the better'.

TORRENCE TESTS

Torrence's tests of creative thinking (see above) were developed to assess the ability of the subject to think divergently and originally. The success of the test-taker will express itself through the divergent thinking facts of: (1) fluency; (2) flexibility; (3) originality; (4) elaboration.

1. FLUENCY expresses itself in the speed and ease with which the test-taker can produce creative ideas, whether they come naturally, or not, and in a flowing style.

2. FLEXIBILITY represents the test-taker's ability to produce different kinds of ideas; the ability to shift from one approach to another, using a rich variety of strategies.

3. ORIGINALITY represents the ability to produce ideas that are unusual, unique, and far-removed from what is normal or commonplace. A person scoring highly in originality may be perceived as non-conforming, but this does not mean that such a person is either erratic or impulsive.

On the contrary, originality is frequently the result of considerable 'controlled' intellectual energy, and it generally shows a capacity for high levels of concentration. The original thinker is more likely to be a 'Renegade from the Norm'.

4. ELABORATION: according to Torrence, high scores on elaboration indicate that the subject is able to develop, embroider, embellish, carry out or otherwise elaborate on ideas. Such persons are likely to demonstrate keenness or sensitivity in observation.

The highest registered scores in the world to date are those of Tony Buzan, who achieved an originality score of 100 per cent, and over all four assessed categories in general scored three times higher than the normal register. In preparation for his Torrence test, Tony Buzan, like Kasparov, trained himself physically, and honed his Mind Mapping and memory skills before breaking the world record.

Creativity, like any other mental skill, can be taught and learned.

CHALLENGE YOURSELF: TRY THESE AT HOME

Here is a selection of challenges tried by the World Memory Champions. Time yourself against the clock. The time available in the championship is given in brackets.

RANDOM WORDS (15 MINUTES)

(Get a friend to help you with these, acting as an examiner, if you want to try them at home.)

Random words are presented in numbered columns of 50. Contestants need to recall words in sequence by writing them down. The columns are scored as follows: no mistakes scores 50 points, one mistake scores 25 points and more than one mistake scores zero points. The column scores are totalled for an overall result.

SPOKEN NUMBER (30 MINUTES)

Contestants recall this number by writing it down. The score is considered as the number of digits from 100 read out, correctly recalled, before a mistake is made. The procedure is repeated three times – only the best score counting.

ONE-HOUR CARD RECALL (1 HOUR)

Contestants are given one hour to memorize as many of 12 packs of cards as they can. No mistakes in a pack of cards scores 52 points. One mistake scores 26 points, and more than one mistake scores zero points.

SPEED CARD RECALL (5 MINUTES)

Contestants are handed a pack of cards shuffled by the arbiter. Stopwatches are set to zero and started in synchrony. When contestants have finished memorizing the pack, they raise their hand and the watch is stopped. Contestants score only as much of the pack as they correctly recall – for example, remembering the whole pack in one minute, but failing on the 25th card, scores 24 points.

POEM (15 MINUTES)

Contestants are given 40 lines of text to memorize from a poem specially written for the event by Ted Hughes, the Poet Laureate. They then recall this text by writing it down, including the punctuation. If a contestant makes any error in a line, that line is scored as zero. A perfect line scores as one point. The specially written poem follows, so that you can try it for yourself!

Memory Champions, such as Dominic O'Brien and Jonathan Hancock, regularly score 100 per cent within the allotted time in such tests – the main exception being the poetry, which tends to be the most difficult to recall.

This poem, deliberately constructed to be difficult to remember, was used for the poetry competition at the World Memory Championship in London in 1995.

THE BLACKENED PEARL

A charred and cheeky jackdaw, no respecter
Of rank or person, is pecking the heart
off your epaulette. And grinding his teeth
A sleeper tries to wake. A city of torches
Casts the black and blacker shadow
Of a beast with two backs
Into his fiery eyes. See, the dark sea
Is moving like a fleet, sinister
Under its flag of sky with a star
And a crescent moon. An African witch
Has danced a pentacle
In the dew. And a father blindfolded,
Wobbles like a top inside it, reaching
Into empty air to catch
His dodgy daughter. He offers her a purse
Crammed with Venetian ducats
And the family pearls. A black hand
Snatches it off him. A man with a cloven hoof,

Masked as a devil, hurries away
Carrying a donkey. See, the sea-thunder
Tosses ashore a chest that spills treasures,
Cod's heads and salmon's tails. But the spider
Hauling its net, finds what it hoped for — a fly!
He contorts his mask, he is not seasick.
Belly-full of poisons he conducts
The drinking and singing till two drunkards
Roll a huge bell down hill.
A devil in black jumps out of it, furious,
Flogs everybody with the rags of a bagpipe
Then calls for perfect silence — which appears
As a bride in a nightgown.
A hawk on her shoulder
Slips away, behind a hedge, and leaves her
Feeding a roasted fowl to a green-eyed monster.
A toad, chewed and spewed out,
Crawls on to her handkerchief and squats,
Masticating strawberries. A tooth
Runs through the house in its sleep
Screaming with pain and babbling secrets.
Two men kneel to pray in a flash of lightning —
They are like two mummies hands wiping the sweat
Off each other with a napkin. Like a raven
Sitting on a cataleptic. Like a dog
Champing and swallowing a nose. Like an eye
Weeping a tear of burning sulphur. Now the whole world,
A pearl pendant between breasts,
Goes under honeysuckle, all are drugged with the scent.
Even the honeysuckle feels drowsy
As a gloved hand pulls out a sword
In the shade of a willow, and a man falls,

Hit by a dove. A red rose, full open
Deepens to black, then pales.
A bed, steered by two dead women,
Tilts over the brink of a cataract
Of liquid flame. The black hand salutes us
Flings a pearl into the pool of fire
Then plunges after it, where a salamander,
Green-eyed and the size of a crocodile,
Swirls in the unplumbed blaze, grabbing the bodies –
Their innocence and their guilt equally spicy.

TED HUGHES

WHAT SHOULD I DO NOW?

1. Learn a mind sport, such as chess, 'Go' or bridge. You can either play against friends or competitively, or you can treat the games as 'logic problems' (solving positions in newspapers and magazines) in order to exercise your 'little grey cells'.
2. Hone your memory skills – remember, we describe the classical memory techniques of memory theatres in Chapter Eleven (page 125).
3. Develop original perspectives on problems or questions that are facing you. Use the associative power of Mind Maps to give you new slants and angles

BRAIN FLASH

GAMES SKILLS IMPORTANT TO BUSINESS

'Skill at backgammon, bridge or chess may well get you further along the career path than your college degree or social connections… excellence in playing games of skill is a reasonably accurate predictor of success – perhaps more accurate than a Harvard MBA.

Whether the game is bridge, backgammon or chess, at the top levels of play the skills rewarded are all vitally important in business. Among them are: discipline, memory, coolness under pressure, psychological insightfulness, a readiness to stick to strategy, even when it produces losing streaks in the short run, and rapid intuitive calculation of probabilities – of spotting opportunities and balancing risks against rewards.'

and to unleash the untapped reservoirs of your own creative force — fresh ideas will then flow freely.

4. Try our memory tests, asking a friend or relation to help or invigilate, especially on the Random Words test.

5. If you are remembering one pack of cards for the first time, here is a hint: use the classical memory technique — for instance, a theatre or a journey — and assign each card a personality and a part to play. Then flip through the deck and weave the cards into your narrative.

CHAPTER FOURTEEN

OPEN FRONTIERS:
VISIONS OF THE FUTURE

———

'YOU CANNOT FIGHT AGAINST THE FUTURE. TIME IS ON OUR SIDE.'

WILLIAM GLADSTONE

INTRODUCTION

So far in *The Age Heresy* we have concentrated on you as an individual. In this final chapter we make our predictions for the future, based on our analysis of the direction in which society – with you as an individual in it – is going to progress.

We look at varying Visions of the Future: prematurely enforced retirement and the failure of the State to provide for the elderly, balanced against ongoing self-reliance and triumphs of technology over seemingly natural human limitations. We even examine the perhaps mixed blessing of the possibility of virtual immortality, through nano-technology and genetic engineering. We show that the frontiers are not, in fact, closing in, but are increasingly opening up – and all you have to do is take advantage of the opportunities that arise and continually stimulate yourself to achieve your full potential.

BRAIN FLASH

A VISION OF THE FUTURE...
'Spectacular advances in medicine and technology. The elimination of most life-threatening cancers through the mapping of human DNA... Women being able to give birth well into their seventies...'

OPEN FRONTIERS: THE EXPONENTIALLY CHANGING FUTURE

We are living in a world of dramatically accelerating change. It took thousands of millions of years for primaeval bacteria in the globigerina ooze of the first oceans to evolve into animal life-forms. It then took hundreds of millions of years for dinosaurs to develop, rule the Earth and vanish. It has taken maybe a couple of million years for humans and human culture to establish themselves, but, incredibly, it is only in the last 200 years or so that we have created anything faster than the horse or sail-power. Over the last half-century scientific developments have come at breakneck speed: first, the discovery of nuclear energy; then, in the past three decades, travel to the moon. And it is only in the most recent period of time that we have started to understand the workings of our own brains.

Ever more speedy change is promised in the forthcoming patterns of our social existence, in medicine, economics, environmental and military matters. We can even aspire now, through the workings of nano-technology, to alter systems at the molecular level, to rearrange matter and rewrite genetic codes.

In this chapter we examine some visions of the future, and look at the risks and challenges that it may hold for an ageing population.

First, here are some views expressed by Professor Marvin Minsky, of the Massachusetts Institute of Technology (MIT). Professor Minsky is widely acknowledged as one of the Patriarchs of AI (Artificial – or Machine – Intelligence). We spoke to him in Boston during 1994, when he opened the second Man v. Machine World Draughts Championship, which the co-authors organized, between Dr Marion Tinsley and the Chinook computer program.

IMMORTALITY: POSSIBLE AND DESIRABLE?

According to Professor Minsky:

'Everyone wants wisdom and wealth, but our bodies may give out before we achieve them. To lengthen our lives, and improve our minds, we'll need to transform our bodies and brains. To that end, we first must see how normal Darwinian evolution brought us to where we are. Then we can look to future techniques to obtain replacements for worn body parts, to solve most problems of failing health. Next, we'll seek wisdom by augmenting our brains and, eventually, by replacing them – with the use of nano-technology. Then, once delivered from the limitations of biology, we'll have to decide on the lengths of our lives – with the option of immortality – as well as to choose among other, unimagined capabilities. In such a future, attaining wealth will not be a problem: the trouble will be controlling it.

'Obviously, such changes are hard to envision, and many thinkers still argue that such advances are impossible – particularly in the domain of artificial intelligence. But the sciences needed to enact this transition are already in the making, and it's time to consider what this new role will be like.

HEALTH AND LONGEVITY

'In recent times we've learnt a lot about health and how to maintain it. We have thousands of specific ways to treat particular diseases and disabilities. However, we do not seem to have increased the length of our maximum life-span.

'Benjamin Franklin lived for 84 years, and, except in popular legends, no one has ever lived twice that long. According to the estimates of Roy Walford, Professor of Pathology at UCLA Medical School, the average human life-span was about 22 years in ancient Rome, about 50 in the developed countries in 1900 and today stands at about 75. Still, the peaks on each curve seem to terminate sharply near 115 years. **Centuries of improvements in health care have had no effect on a recorded maximum of 120.**

Jeanne Calment is the only person to have surpassed this, but our life spans do seem to be limited. Why? Professor Minsky continued:

'The answer is simple. Natural selection favours the genes of those with the most descendants. Those numbers tend to grow exponentially with the number of generations — and so this favours the genes of those who reproduce at earlier ages. Furthermore, evolution does not usually favour genes that lengthen lives beyond the amount adults need to care for their young. Indeed, it may even favour offspring who do not have to compete with living parents. Such competition could even promote the accumulation of genes that cause death.

The Octopus Opportunity

'For example, after spawning, the Mediterranean octopus promptly stops eating and starves to death. If we remove a certain gland, though, the octopus continues to eat, and lives twice as long. Many other animals are programmed to die soon after they cease reproducing. Exceptions to this include those long-lived animals, like ourselves and the elephants, whose progeny learn so much from the social transmission of accumulated knowledge.

'We humans appear to be the longest-lived warm-blooded animals. What selective pressure might have led to our present longevity? **This is related to wisdom!** Among all mammals, our infants are the most poorly equipped to survive by themselves. Hence, we need our parents to care for us and to pass on survival tips. Why do we tend to live twice as long as our other primate relatives? Perhaps because our helplessness became so extreme that **we needed the wisdom of grandparents, too.**

'Whatever the unknown future may bring, already we're changing the rules that made us [a point reinforcing Dr Suzuki's investigations, which we quote on page 3]. Although most of us will be fearful of change, others will surely want to escape from our present limitations. I tried out these ideas on several groups and had them respond to informal polls. I was amazed to find that at least three-quarters of the audience were opposed to the prospect of much longer lives. Many people seemed to feel that our life-spans were already too long. "Why would anyone want to live for five hundred years?" "Wouldn't it be boring?" "What if you

> ## BRAIN FLASH
>
> ### ANOTHER VISION OF THE FUTURE...
> 'The vision of an increasingly dependent elderly population making unsustainable demands on public spending haunts the Western world. In Britain as well as Germany, Japan, America, France and Italy, the assumption is that, some time beyond the turn of the century, there will be too few people in work to support the ever bigger, older and frailer group of pensioners. Either taxes will have to rise, or pensions will have to fall, if government debt is to remain manageable.'
>
> The answer, surely, on the individual personal level, as Sir Brian Tovey would have it, is to set up your own business and **never retire**.

outlived all your friends?" "What would you do with all that time?"

'My scientist friends showed few such concerns. "There are countless things that I want to find out, and so many problems I want to solve, that I could use many centuries." Certainly, immortality would seem unattractive if it meant endless infirmity, debility and dependency upon others – but we're assuming a state of perfect health.'

Fascinating insights from a top scientist, at the cutting-edge of current thinking about ageing. Now we examine other visions of the future.

PREDICTIONS FOR THE FUTURE
(based on conclusions from major UK pension and life-insurance companies)

Traditional work patterns are changing. The company is no longer your 'father', and the concept of cradle-to-grave employment at one company is already fast disappearing. Suppliers of retirement gold watches are going to have a thin time. Only one worker in three now has a standard 9–5 job.

In 1970 41 per cent of men worked in manufacturing. Today it's closer to 28 per cent. Over a similar period, the number of people working for large companies (over 500 employees) fell from 43 to 34 per cent. The trend is for part-time working, either paid very poorly (over a million people earn

£2.50 an hour or less) or extremely well. Either way, your employer won't pay your pension contributions, maternity leave or sickness benefits.

The State is no longer your 'mother' – and don't expect it to be! Traditional social welfare is no longer affordable through taxation.

Both main political parties in the UK (Conservative and Socialist) privately agree that the State can no longer afford to fund pensions and health care adequately. The reason can be seen in almost every family: people are living longer. At the beginning of the twentieth century, one person in 700 was over 80. By the middle of the twenty-first century it's expected to be one in seven. The ratio of workers (funding National Health Insurance) to pensioners could fall as low as 3:1.

A survey in *The Independent on Sunday* warned readers to expect 'state pensions, unemployment benefit and long-term health care to be privatized, and make provision for yourself.'

BRAIN FLASH

WORKING-LIFE EXPECTANCIES HAVE BEEN TURNED UPSIDE-DOWN BY EARLY ACHIEVERS

'Life begins at 40, and so, for an increasing number of high-flyers, does eminence. We are now witnessing the incredible shrinking career – with many people in their early forties doing jobs that used to be reserved for those in their fifties or sixties. Not only rock stars, tennis players and policemen seem young these days; so do Prime Ministers, Leaders of the Opposition and chief executives of high street banks.

What will these still-youthful chief executives do when they have run out of drive and initiative? Orchestrating a permanent revolution must pall after a decade or so at the top, but they will be way off retirement age. They will not have had the wedge-shaped careers that their fathers experienced: gradual promotion from their twenties to their sixties, followed by sudden retirement. The new shape of careers is triangular, with an apex in the middle.

How people cope with the downward slope will vary enormously. Some will be delighted to have the opportunity to pursue interests that they never could before. Some might make a decent living from consultancy, part-time chairmanship and directorships: the "portfolio" approach to work.

Others, however, may become bitter: "The problem is that most people can't get off the moving staircase until they fall off it. Sometimes they're concerned about the loneliness of retirement and they don't have enough to do. That prospect is very frightening."'

You'll switch jobs often – so develop your own versatility. As the current jargon has it, you'll have a portfolio of skills. In your bag will surely be improved computer literacy and a language or two. You'll still specialize, but in a spread of subjects. Marketing executives will be vulnerable if, say, they restrict their knowledge to the motor industry; they would be better off adding skills in office equipment and computers, too. The suggestion is that you'll be employed on demand for perhaps a year or two, then out of work for a while – sometimes at your choosing, in the form of a career break.

Houses – will you rent or buy? You'll still want to buy your own home, but you may well rent for longer before you have children. And when you do buy, you'll be wary of mortgaging yourselves to the hilt. You'll look for green space, which will increasingly command a premium. And communication technology link-ups will be almost as critical as trains and buses.

The good news – you'll live longer. Men can now expect to live on average to 74, and women to 80, although obviously many of us will live far longer. In the future that average will extend itself to an as yet unknown age. And in general you'll lose weight, eat healthier foods (less sugar and dairy produce, more salads and fresh fruit) and take more exercise.

The overall trend is clearly towards greater personal self-reliance.

CONCLUSION

—

We have reached the conclusion of this book and it is time to summarize our message. Over the course of the preceding chapters we have shown you how your brain circuitry can physically improve as you age, how your memory need not fail with increasing years – indeed, it can (and should) improve. We have demonstrated important mental fitness techniques, such as TEFCAS, meta-positive thinking, Mind Mapping and mnemonics, and we have stressed the paramount importance of self-challenge. We have also introduced you to those Renegades from the Norm who are constantly challenging themselves in later years. **You can do this, too.** This is your future!

How to Design Your Own Ageing Strategy

Remember the single most vital lesson in this book: your brain cells are not inevitably dying off every day. The important point is the interconnectivity between your brain cells, your power to make associations and to learn new things – and this you can multiply continually.

The more your brain is stimulated and challenged, the greater its potential to achieve at any age. The latest medical research also indicates that such stimulation is the best defence you can adopt against Alzheimer's Disease or against strokes.

PRACTICAL STEPS

Look after your physical and mental health. Remember: your brain is connected to your body.

If you smoke, try to cut down and then give up entirely. If you drink heavily, cut down. Have a thorough annual physical check-up. Ask your doctor what your ideal weight is and then work to achieve it. Start physical exercise and achieve greater mental clarity by taking up mind sports such as chess, 'Scrabble', draughts, bridge or 'Go'.

Be aware of the phenomenal power of your own brain. It is the most complex structure that we know of in the universe. Use Mind Maps to harness and deploy your full set of cortical resources and skills – to organize your thoughts, help you to communicate, and improve your memory and recall of important facts and ideas.

Remember: the more you learn, the easier it is to learn more. Follow our simple tips in Chapter Three on speed-reading and improving your memory by the use of mnemonics.

How to Change Your Habits

Mobilize meta-positive thinking and TEFCAS to change yourself for the better, to ditch harmful old habits and acquire good new ones. Use the process: Trial, Event, Feedback, Check, Adjust, Success. Remember the main message of meta-positive thinking: it is never too late to start. This is true whether you are taking up a challenging new mental exercise, such as chess; developing a new skill, such as dancing, or a super-power memory; trying a new form of exercise, sport or martial art; or hoping to cut back on alcohol, cigarettes or over-eating.

In summary, as you age, commit yourself to becoming a Renegade from the Norm.

Next, we have distilled six golden rules from the notable experiences related by Sir Brian Tovey (see page 137) for you to follow as you begin your quest to achieve more – not less – as you get older. Here they are:

The Tovey Solution

1. Keep yourself physically and mentally at a fitness peak.
2. Prepare for change and welcome it.
3. Challenge yourself – be ready to take the leap and re-invent yourself.
4. Have the courage to be your own master – whatever your age.
5. Work with a loving and supportive ally (if possible).
6. Love what you do and do what you love. Never retire!

Truth Versus Misconception

On a piece of blank paper, draw your own image of 'age'.

In surveys conducted during the last 20 years, when tens of thousands of individuals were asked to draw their images of age, 80–100 per cent drew negative images. These same individuals were then asked if they knew anyone of 75 or older who did *not* fit this negative category. Encouragingly (and *not* surprisingly!), virtually everyone in the audience raised his or her hand, indicating that there are millions of individuals who are the 'statistical anomalies' referred to in Chapter Four. These individuals we call Renegades from the Norm.

As you now know full well, the brain is drawn towards the image it perceives. If you therefore view age in a morbid and depressing way, that is the way in which you will subconsciously guide your own life, like a missile heading directly towards its own doom.

If you found yourself drawing a walking stick, a skull and crossbones or a gravestone, circle it, put an exclamation mark by the side and commit that image to your memory as the last time you ever thought of age in this way. Your ideal image would have been a smiling face, a world traveller, a healthy and sensuous individual, an athlete, a mountain climber or a multi-millionaire!

All the questions raised in the introduction to this book have now been answered, and in each case we have recommended accessible, positive, concrete and practical steps – none of them too obscure, abstact or difficult for you, the reader, to achieve. Every one of you who has read the book should have found an inspirational message, one that encourages you to improve with age and that shows, simply and clearly, how you can do it yourself.

THE FINAL STEP: THE INTERNATIONAL BRAIN CLUB

'Resolved by the Senate and House of Representatives of the United States of America in Congress Assembled, that the decade beginning January 1, 1990 hereby is designated the "Decade of the Brain", and the President of the United States is authorized and requested to issue a proclamation calling upon all public officials and the people of the United States to observe such decade with appropriate programs and activities.' Approved 25 July 1989.

Join the International Brain Club to meet others who want to stay alert and improve their mental performance as they age. The International Brain Club was conceived by Tony Buzan in 1973, when he was international editor of the magazine of Mensa. The idea took off, and the Brain Club was born. An office was set up in Bournemouth and, in the winter of 1989–90, the first edition of *Synapsia*, the International Brain Club journal (now known as *Use Your Head/Synapsia* magazine), was published.

The goals of the club are:

1. To encourage the personal development of individual members of the club and their families.
2. To promote the development of a worldwide culture of mental literacy and excellence.
3. To generate funds for the purposes of research into the study of thought processes and the mechanics of thinking in learning, understanding, communication, problem-solving, creativity and decision-making.
4. The dissemination of information and teaching of brain-efficient techniques. The *Use Your Head/Synapsia* magazine helps members keep in touch with Tony Buzan's and Ray Keene's latest research and ideas.

The International Brain Club is designed to nurture *you*, and to assist you in the next leap in evolution: the awareness of intelligence by itself and the knowledge that this intelligence can be nurtured, to astounding advantage. The major areas that it focuses on are memory, speed-reading, Mind Mapping, creative thinking, and learning and study skills.

It is immediately apparent from this list of activities that the International Brain Club's priorities coincide precisely with the recommendations made by Dr Arnold Scheibel, head of UCLA's Brain Research Institute, as to how to strengthen the mind and build new brain circuitry (see Chapter Thirteen).

Members of the International Brain Club can be 'individual' members, working on their own personalized programme, or they can meet together at local 'cells' or clubs. Many such clubs have been established, usually meeting on a fortnightly or monthly basis. Meetings are held in the homes of members, at community centres, schools, offices or universities, or in any appropriate environment: places where you can improve, explore and discuss any area of mental literacy development, where you can meet people with the same goals and interests as yourself, make new friends and have lots of fun.

Sometimes experts and lecturers are brought in to talk to a cell, or practical work is undertaken, like that at the Central London Cell, where Mind Mapping and memory practice sessions take place every month.

If you would like further information on any of the above, or would like to join the club, please write to us at:

The International Brain Club
PO Box 1821
Marlow
Bucks SL7 2YW
United Kingdom
E-mail/Internet address: http://www.gold.net:80/users/dx61
Tel: +44(0) 1628 477004

'Brain of the Year' Award – How to Enter

The Brain Trust will be delighted to receive entries and/or nominations from readers for its 'Brain of the Year' Award, and it will also help with the preparation of programmes, articles and competitions surrounding this annual event. For further information please contact:

The Brain Trust
8 Cresswell Gardens
London SW5 OBJ
United Kingdom
Tel. 0171-373 4457
Fax 0171-373 8673

Tony Buzan's Mental Literacy Quest

Surveys have been taken to estimate how many people have heard of the idea of Mind Mapping and, although these have not yet been concluded, we already know that it is in excess of 200 million. Tony Buzan's goal is to have 10 per cent of the planet mentally literate by the beginning of 1999. He is therefore always interested in ideas for helping more people become aware of the concept of Mind Mapping. If anybody has any ideas, he would be delighted to hear from them. You can write to him at the address given on page 175 for the International Brain Club.

FURTHER READING
AND BIBLIOGRAPHY
—

The reading list is designed to give you a wide range of reading material that will introduce you to new perspectives on your brain.

The books have been divided into the following main sections for your ease of reference:
1. Application and Practical
2. Business
3. Education
4. Literature
5. Mind and Body
6. Perspectives
7. The Brain Physiology and Psychology
8. Special Books and Mind Sports

APPLICATION AND PRACTICAL
Buzan, Tony, *Speed Memory*, Newton Abbot: David & Charles (1976)
— *Speed Reading*, Newton Abbot: David & Charles (1976)
— *Make the Most of Your Mind*, London: Pan (1981)
— *The Brain User's Guide*, New York: E.P. Dutton (1983)
— *Use Your Perfect Memory*, New York: E.P. Dutton (1984), Viking Penguin NAL (1990)
— *Harnessing the Parabrain*, London: Wyvern Business Books (1988)

— *Master Your Memory*, London: BBC Books (1989)

— *Use Your Head*, London: BBC Books (1989). Also published as *Use Both Sides of Your Brain*, New York: E.P. Dutton, Viking Penguin NAL (1990)

— *Use Your Memory*, London: BBC Books (1989)

— *The Mind Map Book: Radiant Thinking*, London: BBC Books (1993)

— and Keene, Raymond, *Buzan's Book of Genius*, London: Stanley Paul (1994)

De Bono, Edward, *Lateral Thinking: A Textbook of Creativity*, London: Penguin (1971)

— *Six Thinking Hats*, London: Penguin (1984)

Eysenck, H.J, *Know Your Own IQ*, London: Penguin (Pelican) (1962)

Gelb, Michael, *Present Yourself*, London: Aurum Press (1988)

— and Buzan, Tony, *Lessons from the Art of Juggling*, London: Aurum Press (1995)

Huxley, A., *The Art of Seeing*, New York: Prentice Hall (1975). A book based on the work of W.H. Bates, indicating that the eyes can be 'trained away' from societal-based malfunctioning.

Serebriakoff, V., *How Intelligent Are You?*, New York: New American Library (1968)

Wilson, Glenn, *Improve Your IQ*, London: Futura (1974)

BUSINESS

Drucker, Peter F., *Innovation and Entrepreneurship*, London: Pan (1970)

Naisbitt, John, *Megatrends 2000*, London: Sidgwick & Jackson, New York: William Morrow (1990)

Roberts, Wess, *Leadership Secrets of Attila the Hun*, New York: Warner Books (1989)

Townsend, R., *Up the Organisation*, London: Coronet (1976)

EDUCATION

Devi, Shakuntala, *Figuring – The Joy of Numbers*, London: André Deutsch (1977)

Gawain, S., *Creative Visualisation*, Toronto: Bantam (1978)

Kandel, E. R. and Schwartz, J.H., *Molecular Biology of Learning: Modulation of Transmitter Release, Science*, vol.218, pp.433–43 (1982)

Reid, G., *Accelerated Learning: Technical Training Can Be Fun, Training & Development Journal*, vol.39 (9), pp.24–7 (1985)

Robinson, A.D., *What You See is What You Get, Training & Development Journal*, vol.38 (5), pp.34–9 (1984)

Trachtenberg, J., *Speed System of Basic Mathematics*, London: Souvenir Press (1989)

LITERATURE

Borges, L., *Fictions*, London: Calder Jupiter Books (1965) (especially 'Funes, the Memorious')

Kawabata, Yasunari, *The Master of Go*, London: Penguin (1976)

Saint-Exupéry, Antoine de, *The Little Prince*, London: Heinemann (1991), New York: Harcourt Brace Jovanovich (1971)

MIND AND BODY

Alexander, F.M., *The Use of the Self*, London: Thames & Hudson (1974)

Bates, W.H., *Better Eyesight Without Glasses*, New York: Mayflower

Carper, Jean, *Stop Aging Now!: The Amazing Anti-aging Powers of Supplements, Herbs and Food*, New York, HarperCollins (1995)

Gelb, Michael, *Body Learning*, London: Aurum Press (1986)

PERSPECTIVES

Bergamini, D., *The Universe*, Amsterdam: Time Life Series (1974). A poetic, colourful and brilliantly illustrated description of the Universe, giving many useful analogies for the increasing dimensions of our knowledge about the brain.

Chopra, Deepak, *Ageless Body, Timeless Mind*, New York: Harmony Books (1993)

Crawford, Prof. Michael and Marsh, David, *Driving Force: Food Evolution and the Future*, London: Heinemann

Hooper, J. and Teresi, D., *The Three-Pound Universe*, New York: Dell Publishing (1986)

Howe, M.J.A., *Using Students' Notes to Examine the Role of the Individual Learner in Acquiring Meaningful Subject Matter*, Journal of Educational Research, vol.64, pp.61–3

— and Godfrey, J., *Student Note-Taking as an Aid to Learning*, Exeter: Exeter University Teaching Services (1977)

Hunt, E., *How Good Can Memory Be? Encoding processes in human memory*, edited by A.W. Melton and E. Martin, Washington, DC: Winston/Wiley, pp.237–60 (1972)

Hunter, I.M.L., *An Exceptional Memory*, British Journal of Psychology, vol.68, pp.155–64 (1977)

Leavitt, Harold J., *Managerial Psychology*, Chicago: University of Chicago Press (1978)

Luria, A., *Mind of a Mnemonist*, London: Jonathan Cape (1969). The original work by the psychologist who studied the mind of Shereshevsky, the Russian with the perfect memory. Should be read not only as a case history but also as a manual.

THE BRAIN PHYSIOLOGY AND PSYCHOLOGY

Haber, Ralph, *How We Remember What We See*, Scientific American, vol.105 (May 1970)

Ornstein, Robert., *The Psychology of Consciousness*, London: Penguin, New York: Harcourt Brace Jovanovich (1977). The original work by Ornstein on his researches with Roger Sperry and others into the left and right hemispheres of the brain, including many pertinent comments on the applications of the research to the individual and society.

Penfield, W. and Perot, P., *The Brain's Record of Auditory and Visual Experience: A Final Summary and Discussion*, Brain, vol.86, pp.595–702

— and Roberts, L., *Speech and Brain-Mechanisms*, Princeton, NJ: Princeton University Press (1959)

Reystak, R.M., *The Mind*, Toronto: Bantam (1988)

Robertson-Tchabo, E.A., Hausman, C.P. and Arenberg, D., *A Classical Mnemonic for Older Learners: A Trip That Works*, in *Adult Development & Ageing*, Boston: Little, Brown (1982)

Russel, Peter, *The Brain Book*, London: Routledge & Kegan Paul (1979). The history of the psychological research that led to the development of the Brain Club/Use Your Head Club idea, and based on the original research done by Tony Buzan.

Schaie, K.W. and Geiwitz, J., *Adult Development & Ageing*, Boston: Little, Brown (1982)

Serebriakoff, Victor, *Guide to Intelligence and Personality Testing*, New York: New American Library (1968)

Standing, Lionel, *Learning 10,000 Pictures*, Quarterly Journal of Experimental Psychology, vol.25, pp.207–22

Walsh, D.A., *Age Differences in Learning & Memory*, in *Ageing: Scientific Perspectives and Social Issues*, Monterey, California: Books/Cole Publishing (second edition 1975)

Yates, F.A., *The Art of Memory*, London: Routledge & Kegan Paul (1966), Ark (1984)

SPECIAL BOOKS AND MIND SPORTS

Boorman, Scott A., *The Protracted Game*, Oxford: Oxford University Press (1971). An interpretation of Mao Tse-Tung's military strategy as a gigantic game of 'Go'.

Burke, James, *The Day the World Changed*, London: BBC Books (1981)

Carroll, Lewis, Alice in Wonderland (playing cards)

Carroll, Lewis, Alice Through the Looking Glass (chess)

Keene, Raymond, *Chess for Absolute Beginners*, London: Batsford (1993)

— *Kingfisher Pocket Book of Chess*, London: Kingfisher (1994)

— and Divinsky, Nathan, *Warriors of the Mind*, London: Hardinge Simpole Publishing (1989)

— and Kasparov, Garry, *Batsford Chess Openings for Two*, London: Batsford (1993)

SOURCES OF 'BRAIN FLASHES'

——

p.VIII *Successful Ageing: Perspectives from the Behavioural Sciences,* Paul B. and Margaret M. Baltes, Cambridge University Press, 1993

p.5 *International Herald Tribune,* 1 March 1994

p.7 Graham Sarjeant in *The Times,* 1994

p.14 *The Times,* 29 September 1994

p.20 *The Independent on Sunday Review,* 21 May 1995

p.23 *International Herald Tribune,* 1995

p.46 *USA Today,* 9 May 1995

p.48 UCLA's Brain Research Institute, July 1994

p.51 National Institute of Ageing, 1 March 1984

p.52 *Competitive Advantage Through Diversity,* Peter Herriot and Carole Pemberton

p.64 *Life* Magazine, July 1994

p.72 *Time* Magazine, 6 March 1995

p.75 *The Times,* 22 February 1995

p.92 *Journal of the American Medical Association,* May 1995

p.99 *The Observer,* 9 October 1994

p.99 *The European* magazine, May 1995

p.101 *Time* Magazine, July 1995

p.104 *The Times,* 12 May 1995

p.112 *Life* Magazine, July 1994

p.119 K.W. Schaie and J. Geiwitz, 1982

p.136 *The Independent,* 1 October 1994

p.138 *The Times,* 17 May 1995

p.140 *The Times,* 28 January 1995

p.143 *The Times,* 1 July 1995

p.143 *Personnel Today,* 25 May 1995

p.145 *The Sunday Times*, 26 June 1995

p.146 *Life* Magazine, July 1994

p.151 *International Herald Tribune*, 1 March 1984

p.162 *Forbes* Magazine, 13 March 1995

p.164 *Tomorrow's World* BBC TV series, 7 July 1995

p.168 *The Times*, leading article, 21 June 1995

pp.168–70 Predictions based on those by experts from Scottish Amicable, quoted in *The Times*, May 1995.

p.169 *The Times*, 1 October 1994

FURTHER INFORMATION

ALSO BY RAYMOND KEENE, OBE

You can read Grand Master Raymond Keene on chess every day in *The Times* of London and each week in *The Spectator*. Among the world-record 85 books he has written on chess and mind sports in general, the following are particularly recommended:

Batsford Chess Openings II This is the standard one-volume reference work on chess openings. Since the first edition was published in 1982, the book has sold more than 100,000 copies. The co-author is the World Chess Champion, Garry Kasparov.

Chess for Absolute Beginners The ideal introduction to chess, perfect for children and adults alike, with simple, clear and easy-to-understand diagrams in colour by artist Barry Martin.

Buzan's Book of Genius, and How to Unleash Your Own Written by Tony Buzan with Raymond Keene. All the advice you need to fulfil your potential and make the most of your mental skills.

ALSO BY TONY BUZAN

The Mind Map Book: Radiant Thinking The comprehensive guide to Mind Mapping™ by its originator. Exciting new ways to use and improve your memory, concentration and creativity in planning and structuring thought on all levels.

Use Your Head The classic BBC bestseller, which has sold over a million copies. Foundation learning skills and Mind Mapping explained by their inventor. Latest information on your brain's functioning, enabling you to Learn How to Learn more effectively.

Use Your Memory An encyclopaedia of brain-related memory techniques. Provides easy-to-manage techniques for remembering names, faces, places, jokes, telephone numbers and everything you want or need to remember.

Speed/Range Reading Establish a range of reading speeds up to 10,000 wpm with good comprehension. Self-checks and practical exercises throughout.

Make the Most of Your Mind (paperback); *Harnessing the Parabrain* (hardback). A complete course-in-book dealing with reading, memory number skills, logic, vision, listening and study. Builds to the complete Mind Map Organic Study Technique.

To make the most of your Mind at any age, contact the one stop shop for all brain-related courses and products, Buzan Centres, 54 Parkstone Road, Poole, Dorset, UK BH15 2PX; Tel: +44(0) 1202 533593; Fax: +44(0) 1202 534572 or E mail: 101737.1141@compuserve.com

Or at 415 Federal Highway, Lake Park, Florida 33403 USA. Tel: +1(407) 881 0188; Fax: +1(407) 845 3210; E mail: Buzan000@aol.com